500+ HAPPENINGS TO PROVE EXISTENCE

and how to use them in your writing

AN EXPERIMENTAL PLAY ON WORDS

with Laura Grebe and Reji Laberje

Quantity order requests can be emailed to:
publishing@rejilaberje.com

Or mailed to:
Reji Laberje Writing and Publishing
Publishing Orders
234 W. Broadway Street
Waukesha, WI 53186

Grebe, Laura
500+ Happenings to Prove Existence
Contributing Author: Reji Laberje
Contributing Editor: Reji Laberje
Cover Design: Michael Nicloy
Interior Layout: Reji Laberje

ISBN-13: 978-1945907067

ISBN-10: 1945907061

SALES Categories:
Reference / Writing, Research & Publishing Guides / Writing
Humor & Entertainment / Humor / Puns & Wordplay
Reference / Dictionaries & Thesauruses / Synonyms & Antonyms

BISAC Codes:
LAN021000Language Arts & Disciplines / Vocabulary
LAN005000Language Arts & Disciplines / Composition & Creative Writing
HUM019000Humor / Topic / Language

Writing and Publishing
www.rejilaberje.com

Dedication

For all the creative individuals and supporting family and friends who didn't know it at the time but gave me the idea for some of this stuff while stuck on the couch. For Maddy and Noah for being the root cause of me being stuck on the couch...or maybe that's Josh.

500+

Happenings

500+ Happenings

500+

Happenings

500+ HAPPENINGS

500+

500+ Happenings

Happenings

Foreword

I think I was somewhere in the middle of binge watching "Criminal Minds" or "The Walking Dead" when I decided that even though I was stuck on the couch and my situation was less than ideal, I still had to do something during the day or I was going to go crazy.

I had just entered the second trimester of a rather stressful pregnancy and was put on modified home bed rest (aka – couch rest). I went from running three miles every morning and spending long days at the office to spending 90% of my time in bed or lying on the couch and wearing pajamas or sweats all day. I was in a funk, and rightfully so if I do say so myself.

*What it was I saw or thought while watching another helpless victim beg uselessly for mercy or a group of staggering, limping zombies viciously attack a group of strong able-bodied adults, I'm not sure. Maybe it was just a sudden understanding that the world wasn't going to stop just because I was stopped. Maybe it was the realization that the fictional characters in the shows I was watching had it way worse than me and they **still needed to live**. Maybe it was my own sanity breaking through and telling me to shape up. Whatever it was, I knew I needed to do something or I was going to go crazy.*

*But exactly what **can** you do when stuck on the couch? I made a list of what I already did that day, because I have a personality for which lists are therapeutic. I breathed. Yeah; did that. I put on a t-shirt in place of my long-sleeved PJ top (I had pregnant-lady heat stroke). I watched TV. I talked (to my spider friend), texted (my Mum), checked Facebook ('Who else is having problems today?' 'Is there a mind-numbing quiz I can do to kill 5 minutes?'), drank water, and ate lunch (gotta feed and water the tiny human growing in there!) I realized that I did actually accomplish things during the day. I participated in life.*

I existed.

My remaining time on the couch ended up not being that bad. And yes, I was on couch rest until the day the tiny human got evicted.

Don't we all have days when we're not sure what we've accomplished? Moments when you're just in a funk and don't feel like doing anything? Every single person goes through a time when all you want to do is sit on the couch or stay in bed and watch the world . . . without participating. Whether it's depression, illness, anxiety, exhaustion, grief, sorrow, agony, pain, doctor-ordered, or what have you, we all have days, weeks, months, or even years like that. Eventually, though, we all have to join the world again and participate. We all exist even when we don't feel like it.

This list is proof!

~Laura

About this Book

Laura works with Reji Laberje Writing and Publishing for her Experimental Word Play books and other publications.

We have an awesome online place with cool stuff . . . video, audio, downloadables and social media mayhem. You can learn about Laura, her books, really wicked awesome stuff like these lists, and so much more!

We call it her "Electronic Resource Hub", or, ERH.

I personally can't wait to see what happens. Laura's like our own personal grammar girl . . . but with word banks – Word Girl!

In fact, if you check back, and back, and back, we'll be adding, and adding, and adding to it. You'll find—not just really cool Experimental Word Play stuff from "Happenings", "Verbal Emojis", and "Still Useful Words", but also her upcoming "Cupcake Therapy" book, a maternity journal like no other, and eventually books ranging from children's mysteries to Patent Law?

Yeah.
We know.
She's pretty flipping impressive.
We love her, too!

At any rate, you can visit Laura Grebe's ERH by scanning the code below with your smart device or typing in the website on your chosen browser. Check out all those cool ERH goodies and a bunch of other useful knowledge on her publisher's site.

When you do give in to the digital peer pressure, we say "Thanks", "Merci", "Gracias", and—of course—"Danke" for dropping by!

Yours in writing,
Reji Laberje and Laura's Publishing Team!

Laura Grebe – Electronic Resource Hub
www.rejilaberje.com/laura-grebe.html

What's Happening?

The Happenings List   1

Word Play . . . Your Happenings List   9

The Happenings Dictionary   12

Word Play . . . Your Happenings Dictionary   36

The Happenings Thesaurus   40

Word Play . . . Your Happenings Thesaurus   62

The Happenings Categories   66

Thinking Words   68

Doing Words   69

Going Words   75

Word Play . . . Your Happenings Categories   76

The Happenings in Time   79

Time of Day Thinking Words   81

Time of Day Doing Words   84

Time of Day Going Words   87

Word Play . . . Your Happenings in Time   90

The Happenings Characterizations   97

Thinking Characterizations   99

Doing Characterizations   102

Going Characterizations   105

Word Play . . . Your Happenings Characterizations   108

The Happenings Passage   112

Word Play . . . Your Happenings Passage   114

As Promised . . . for Overachievers   116

Afterword   129

Resources & References Consulted   130

About the Authors   131

The difference between the almost right word and the right word is really a large matter - 'tis the difference between the lightning-bug and the lightning.

~Mark Twain

The

Happenings

Happenings

List

Happenings

The

LIST

List

The

"The Happenings List"

The following list is over 500 (503 if you need to be exact) active phrases that people do on a relatively regular basis.

The following list of over 500 (yeah, fine, 503) active phrases are also great things to happen or as a result of your characters in your stories. Even if a character seems sedentary, inactive, unimportant, inconsequential, minor, or trivial – if there is a reason you put a character into a situation, then that character is likely doing something.

These active phrases can add a doing, thinking, or going happening to your character and establish that character's existence in a way that simply describing physical attributes cannot.

Seriously think about this for a minute. Page through the list. Consider yourself.

In any measurable period of time I bet you can put a checkmark next to at least one of these happenings….okay, maybe not actually in any measurable period of time. In any given hour, maybe. In any given hour, I bet you can put a checkmark next to at least one of these happenings. (Yeah, that seems better.) I dare you to try and exist for an hour without putting a check next to at least one of these happenings. In fact, I'm guessing, after a mere hour, you'd probably check off as many as a dozen happenings. But, you may not believe me, so go ahead and try to exist without happening for a full hour.

Did you try? Honestly, you probably didn't, (who has that kind of time these days?!), but you did more than likely THINK about that hour. It's impossible not to have happenings, right?

If it's impossible for you to not exist for an hour, it's impossible for your character – this mental development of yours – this creation of your brain – to exist in the situation you have created without doing at least one of these things.

Let your character exist.

1.	Accept a Compliment	47.	Change Clothes
2.	Accept Responsibility	48.	Check Email
3.	Aerobics	49.	Check Facebook
4.	Agonize	50.	Check for a Bump
5.	Answer a Question	51.	Check the Time
6.	Apologize	52.	Check the Weather
7.	Ask a Question	53.	Check Voicemail
8.	Ask Directions	54.	Cheer
9.	Ask for Help	55.	Chew Gum
10.	Attend a Meeting	56.	Chuckle
11.	Avoid an Accident	57.	Clap
12.	Avoid Someone	58.	Clean
13.	Avoid Something	59.	Clean a Closet
14.	Balance Checkbook	60.	Clean the Bathroom
15.	Be Brave	61.	Clean the Microwave
16.	Be Inappropriate	62.	Clean the Oven
17.	Beep	63.	Clean the Stove
18.	Belch	64.	Clench Your Fists
19.	Bite a Fingernail	65.	Close Your Eyes
20.	Bite Your Lip	66.	Clothes Shopping
21.	Bite Your Nails	67.	Clown Around
22.	Bite Your Tongue	68.	Color
23.	Blink	69.	Complain
24.	Blow dry Hair	70.	Complement Someone
25.	Blow Nose	71.	Compliment Yourself
26.	Blush	72.	Contemplate Life
27.	Boil Water	73.	Contemplate Love
28.	Bow	74.	Correct Someone
29.	Break a Habit	75.	Correct Yourself
30.	Break a Nail	76.	Cough
31.	Break a Promise	77.	Count
32.	Break a Shoe	78.	Count to Ten
33.	Break Something	79.	Crack a Knuckle
34.	Breathe	80.	Crack Your Back
35.	Brush Hair	81.	Crack Your Neck
36.	Brush Teeth	82.	Crave Junk Food
37.	Burn a Candle	83.	Crave Something Weird
38.	Burp	84.	Criticize Someone
39.	Buy Clothes	85.	Critique Something
40.	Call a Different Area Code	86.	Cross the Street
41.	Call a Friend	87.	Cross Your Fingers
42.	Call a Parent	88.	Cross Your Legs
43.	Call a Sibling	89.	Cry
44.	Call Home	90.	Curse
45.	Carry a Purse	91.	Cuss
46.	Change a Light Bulb	92.	Cut Fingernails

93.	Cut Toenails	139.	Entertain
94.	Dance	140.	Exercise
95.	Daydream	141.	Exhale
96.	Delegate	142.	Fart
97.	Deposit a Check	143.	Feel Grass
98.	Dine In	144.	Fib
99.	Dine Out	145.	Fill a Cup
100.	Do Mental Math	146.	Find a Penny
101.	Donate Food	147.	Find Money
102.	Donate Money	148.	Finish a Countdown
103.	Donate Something	149.	Flirt
104.	Donate Time	150.	Fluff Your Pillow
105.	Doodle	151.	Flush
106.	Draw a Portrait	152.	Fly
107.	Dream	153.	Fold Laundry
108.	Dress Down	154.	Follow Instructions
109.	Dress Up	155.	Forget Something
110.	Drink Coffee	156.	Forgive
111.	Drink Juice	157.	Fret
112.	Drink Soda	158.	Frown
113.	Drink Tea	159.	Fuss
114.	Drink Water	160.	Garden
115.	Drive	161.	Get a Hug
116.	Drop Something	162.	Get a Kiss
117.	Drop Your Phone	163.	Get a Surprise
118.	Drum Your Fingers	164.	Get Dressed
119.	Dust	165.	Get a Massage
120.	Dust a Cobweb	166.	Get Scolded
121.	Eat	167.	Get Sick
122.	Eat a Cookie	168.	Get Tickled
123.	Eat a Fruit	169.	Giggle
124.	Eat a Salad	170.	Give a Fist Bump
125.	Eat a Sandwich	171.	Give a Hug
126.	Eat a Snack	172.	Give a Kiss
127.	Eat a Vegetable	173.	Give Directions
128.	Eat Breakfast	174.	Give Instructions
129.	Eat Candy	175.	Glare
130.	Eat Chocolate	176.	Go on a Date
131.	Eat Dessert	177.	Go Outside
132.	Eat Ice Cream	178.	Go to a Concert
133.	Eat Meat	179.	Go to a Movie
134.	Eat Off a Paper Plate	180.	Go to a Party
135.	Eat Outside	181.	Go to Church
136.	Empathize	182.	Go to Work
137.	Empty Trash	183.	Goof Off
138.	Enforce a Rule	184.	Gossip

185.	Grieve	231.	Make a Correction
186.	Grin	232.	Make a Face
187.	Grind Your Teeth	233.	Make a Mess
188.	Grocery Shop	234.	Make a Mistake
189.	Grumble	235.	Make a Promise
190.	Hang Laundry	236.	Make a Sandwich
191.	Have Fun	237.	Make a Wish
192.	Have Sex	238.	Make a Wrong Turn
193.	Help Someone	239.	Make an Animal Noise
194.	Hiccup	240.	Make Coffee
195.	Hit Snooze	241.	Make Dinner
196.	Hold a Door	242.	Make Love
197.	Hold Your Tongue	243.	Make Lunch
198.	Hop	244.	Make Small Talk
199.	Host a Party	245.	Make Someone Else's Bed
200.	Hug	246.	Make Something Up
201.	Imitate Someone	247.	Make Tea
202.	Improvise	248.	Make Toast
203.	Inhale	249.	Make To-Do List
204.	Interrupt Someone	250.	Make Whoopi
205.	Investigate	251.	Make Your Bed
206.	Iron	252.	Make-Out
207.	Itch	253.	Meditate
208.	Jaywalk	254.	Meet a Friend
209.	Jump	255.	Meet Someone New
210.	Keep a Secret	256.	Mind Your Manners
211.	Keep Someone Waiting	257.	Misbehave
212.	Laugh	258.	Miss Someone
213.	Laugh at a Joke	259.	Miss Your Stop
214.	Laugh at Someone	260.	Moan
215.	Laugh at Yourself	261.	Mock
216.	Laundry	262.	Mop
217.	Lead a Meeting	263.	Mow the Lawn
218.	Learn Something New	264.	Nag
219.	Lick a Knife	265.	Nap
220.	Lick Your Fingers	266.	Negotiate
221.	Lie	267.	Nod
222.	Listen to Music	268.	Paint
223.	Listen to the Radio	269.	Pamper Yourself
224.	Lose at Something	270.	Pant
225.	Lose Something	271.	Park a Car
226.	Lose Your Thought	272.	Pass Gas
227.	Love Someone	273.	Pay Bills
228.	Love Yourself	274.	Perform a Ritual
229.	Mail a Letter	275.	Pet Someone
230.	Make a Confession	276.	Pet Something

277.	Pick Your Nose	323.	Say "Hello"
278.	Pinch	324.	Say "Hi"
279.	Pity Yourself	325.	Say "I Love You"
280.	Plan Something	326.	Say "I'm Sorry"
281.	Play a Game	327.	Say "Thank You"
282.	Play an Instrument	328.	Say "You're Welcome"
283.	Plot	329.	Say a Prayer
284.	Plug Your Ears	330.	Say Your Name
285.	Point	331.	Scold Someone
286.	Post to Facebook	332.	Scowl
287.	Praise God	333.	Scratch
288.	Pray	334.	Scream
289.	Prepare Breakfast	335.	Scrub Floors
290.	Prepare Dinner	336.	See a Play
291.	Prepare Lunch	337.	Send Email
292.	Procrastinate	338.	Set Alarm Clock
293.	Pull Weeds	339.	Shake Hands
294.	Put on Jewelry	340.	Shake Your Butt
295.	Put on Make-up	341.	Shake Your Head
296.	Put on Shoes	342.	Shake Your Hips
297.	Put on Socks	343.	Share a Secret
298.	Read	344.	Shave
299.	Read a Book	345.	Shop
300.	Read a Magazine	346.	Shop Online
301.	Read a Menu	347.	Show Up Late
302.	Read a Newspaper	348.	Shower
303.	Read Bible	349.	Sigh
304.	Read Out Loud	350.	Sign Something
305.	Read the News	351.	Sign Your Name
306.	Receive Email	352.	Sign-In
307.	Receive Mail	353.	Sign-Up
308.	Relax	354.	Sin
309.	Reminisce	355.	Sing
310.	Repair Something	356.	Sing in the Car
311.	Repeat Someone	357.	Sing in the Shower
312.	Repeat Yourself	358.	Sit in Traffic
313.	Return a Call	359.	Sketch
314.	Ride an Escalator	360.	Skip
315.	Ride in an Elevator	361.	Slam a Door
316.	Roll Your Eyes	362.	Slip
317.	Rub Tummy	363.	Smell an Herb
318.	Run	364.	Smell Something Gross
319.	Run Errands	365.	Smell Something Nice
320.	Run Late	366.	Smell the Flowers
321.	Rush	367.	Smile
322.	Save Money	368.	Smirk

369.	Snap	415.	Talk to a Neighbor
370.	Sneak	416.	Talk to Your Bump
371.	Sneeze	417.	Talk to Yourself
372.	Snort	418.	Teach Someone Something
373.	Snuggle	419.	Tease Someone
374.	Solve a Puzzle	420.	Tell a Joke
375.	Speak a Different Language	421.	Tell a Lie
376.	Spend Money	422.	Tell a Story
377.	Spill Something	423.	Tell a Truth
378.	Splash	424.	Tell Someone How You Feel
379.	Splurge	425.	Text a Friend
380.	Squint	426.	Text a Parent
381.	Stand in the Shade	427.	Text Partner
382.	Stand in the Sun	428.	Think Bad Thoughts
383.	Start a Countdown	429.	Think Dirty Thoughts
384.	Start a Habit	430.	Think Happy Thoughts
385.	Step in a Puddle	431.	Tickle Someone
386.	Step in Mud	432.	Tidy Up
387.	Stretch	433.	Tie Shoes
388.	Strike a Pose	434.	Tiptoe
389.	Stub Toe	435.	Touch Money
390.	Study	436.	Trip
391.	Surprise Someone	437.	Try a New Food
392.	Swat a Bug	438.	Try on Clothes
393.	Swat a Fly	439.	Try Something New
394.	Swear	440.	Turn Off Lights
395.	Sweat	441.	Turn On Lights
396.	Sweep	442.	Twiddle Thumbs
397.	Swim	443.	Unwind
398.	Swing	444.	Use a Computer
399.	Take a Bath	445.	Use a Credit Card
400.	Take a Break	446.	Use a Napkin
401.	Take a Nap	447.	Use Sign Language
402.	Take a Picture	448.	Vacuum
403.	Take a Selfie	449.	Visit a Different Zip Code
404.	Take a Taxi	450.	Visit a Friend
405.	Take a Test	451.	Visit a Parent
406.	Take a Vitamin	452.	Visit a Relative
407.	Take a Walk	453.	Wait for Someone
408.	Take Notes	454.	Walk
409.	Take Off Clothes	455.	Walk Down Stairs
410.	Take the Subway	456.	Walk in the Crosswalk
411.	Take Your Time	457.	Walk in the Street
412.	Talk About Weather	458.	Walk on a Sidewalk
413.	Talk on Phone	459.	Walk Up Stairs
414.	Talk to a Friend	460.	Wash Dishes

461.	Wash Face	483.	Weep
462.	Wash Hands	484.	Whine
463.	Wash Windows	485.	Whisper
464.	Watch a Commercial	486.	Wiggle Toes
465.	Watch a Movie	487.	Win at Something
466.	Watch a Sport	488.	Window Shop
467.	Watch the News	489.	Wink
468.	Watch the Sunrise	490.	Wish
469.	Watch the Sunset	491.	Work
470.	Watch TV	492.	Workout
471.	Water a Plant	493.	Worry
472.	Wave	494.	Worship
473.	Wear a Coat	495.	Write a Note
474.	Wear a Hat	496.	Write in Colors
475.	Wear a Uniform	497.	Write in Pen
476.	Wear Flip-Flops	498.	Write in Pencil
477.	Wear Jewelry	499.	Write the Date
478.	Wear Pants	500.	Write Your Name
479.	Wear Pantyhose	501.	Yawn
480.	Wear Slippers	502.	Yoga
481.	Wear Sunglasses	503.	Zip a Zipper
482.	Wear Your Fat Pants		

Word
Word Play!
Play
Word Play!
Word
Play
Play

Word
Word Play!

WORD PLAY . . . YOUR Happenings List

Admit it! You started thinking of words and phrases as you went through this list and since you're not me and I'm not you, the words and phrases you thought of may not be in my list. Since these lists of words are all about experimenting with words for your journaling, writing, theatrical endeavors, intellectual stimulation, creativity, or to just prove to all of your friends that you ARE exactly "what's happening", when it comes to word play, take time to create on your *own* word play throughout this book. On this page and the next, extend the list with as many of YOUR Happenings as you can think to add to the already extensive list shared.

504. _____

505. _____

506. _____

507. _____

508. _____

509. _____

510. _____

511. _____

512. _____

513. _____

514. _____

515. _____

516. _____

517. _____

518. _____

519. _____

520. _____

521. _____

522. _____

523. _____

524. _____

525. _____

526. _____

527. _____

528. _____

529. _____

530. _____

531. _____

Need more room? Really? Well, now you're just showing off! It's all good, though. I left blank and lined pages at the back of the book for the overachievers just like you! Phhhttt!

The
Happenings
Dictionary
The
Happenings
Dictionary
The

Dictionary
Happenings

"The Happenings Dictionary"

These definitions were derived from exchanges between professional authors after consulting the Merriam Webster Dictionary, Oxford English Dictionary, and Dictionary.com.

Let's be honest; most of us pretty much use the latter of that list, but not going any further than that is sort of like turning in your college papers with nothing but Wikipedia on your bibliographies. You could be right. OR . . . you could be memorizing the phrase, "Do you want fries with that?"

Besides, we're writers, right? We want to use, and combine, and manipulate words to create the most specific meanings we can. When we do hit those right words, if we're lucky, we are totally freaking out with the amazeballs scenes we create!

(By the way, "freaking" is ONLY listed as a slang intensifier on Dictionary.com, so you can see what I mean! Mind you, they do have the word "amazeballs". What's up with that?)

In short, I've got you a writer's dictionary of happenings, here. Sure, I kept the whole alphabetical thing going on because, you know, OCD (writers, right?), but you're getting more than just the meaning of the happenings, you're getting the definitions AS a writer should use them in his or her writing.

Hey, that's catchy! Maybe that should be a subtitle:

"And How to Use Them in Your Writing"

Yep. Think I'll keep it.

Anyway, here it comes – the dictionary of happenings according to an **Experimental Word Player** . . . kinky!

WORD OR PHRASE	DEFINITION (OR JUST AN AMAZEBALLS NOTE)
Accept a Compliment	Acknowledge one's genuine, positive praise; To receive AND BELIEVE positive (hopefully honest) feedback from another
Accept Responsibility	Acknowledge care for somebody or something; verbally express wrongdoing
Aerobics	Exercise that increases one's respiratory activity; Made famous by poorly chosen 1980s athletic wear
Agonize	To be negatively preoccupied over a person, thought, situation, or concern
Answer a Question	To respond, verbally or in writing, to one's inquiry
Apologize	To say "I'm Sorry"; make an admission of wrongdoing (or perceived wrongdoing)
Ask a Question	To request a response to an unknown inquiry
Ask Directions	Seek physical, step-by-step descriptions of how to reach a destination
Ask for Help	Can be to seek physical or emotional support, but can also be the simple seeking of a listening ear
Attend a Meeting	Go to a proper appointment time, usually for something professional, spiritual, or medical
Avoid an Accident	By intentional swerving or other means, keep oneself out of a collision; or – if you're a three-year-old, cross your legs really tightly and "do the dance"
Avoid Someone	Take intentional physical (and possibly electronic) measures to ensure not making contact with an individual
Avoid Something	Make intentional efforts to keep from doing a task or going to an event (usually of an unpleasant nature)
Balance Checkbook	Align credits and debits in an account for the purpose of coming out even according to expectations; rarely do people do this in an actual "checkbook" these days so much as through an online banking or bookkeeping system
Be Brave	Purposefully confront a situation with a heart of courage in the face of a physical or emotional fear
Be Inappropriate	Dress, speak, or act in a behavior unbecoming to one's expected social status, employment, or personal character
Beep	Depress one's horn, on a car or bicycle, to make a sound of warning, anger, or celebration
Belch	Oral, audible release of gas, usually referring to a relatively large sound; great for family contests around the dinner table to practice the "Be Inappropriate" happening
Bite a Fingernail	The act of chewing on the nails, and skin around the nails, at the end of one's fingers, usually out of stress, frustration, nervousness, or habit
Bite Your Lip	The act of chewing on one's lips, usually peeling away the top layer of skin in the process, done sometimes due to chapping, but also out of stress, frustration, nervousness, or habit

Bite Your Nails	See "Bite a fingernail"; of course, I guess you could be biting the nails on your wall or your toenails, but that's just weird
Bite Your Tongue	Usually while chewing food, to bite down on one's own tongue in his or her mouth; Also what you metaphorically do when you are not speaking your mind despite an itching urge to do wo
Blink	To rapidly close one's eyes and reopen them; usually subconsciously; the average human blinks 28,800 times per day
Blow Dry Hair	With an electric device that expels warm air, take the moisture out of one's hair; cats love this . . . or hate this . . . depends on the cat
Blow Nose	To expel mucus, usually into a tissue; also SNOT ROCKET!
Blush	To have one's cheeks turn a rose color, usually as a result of emotional or physical exertion; also the pinkish powder to create the same effect with makeup
Boil Water	To heat water to a temperature of 212 degrees Fahrenheit (although, in Denver, water boils at 203 degrees Fahrenheit!)
Bow	To bend at the waist as a sign of respect or introduction, or to accept praise at the end of an artistic performance
Break a Habit	To intentionally stop doing something, usually something that has negative implications
Break a Nail	To split or crack a nail, usually on a fingertip; again, I guess you could break a nail in your wall, which would kind of suck, but not as much as breaking a toenail which really sucks
Break a Promise	To not follow-through on a verbalized physical, emotional, or social treaty
Break a Shoe	To damage a piece of footwear, especially in the case of a heel coming off a woman's shoe . . . so annoying
Break Something	To create damage, typically in an irreparable manner
Breathe	The act of inhaling and exhaling, inhaling and exhaling, inhaling and exhaling, inhaling and exhaling . . . where was I?
Brush Hair	Running a multi-bristled item through one's hair to create style, prevent tangles, or – in the case of my curly-haired sisters, tease and frizz
Brush Teeth	Using a small bristled item with cleansing paste to clean one's teeth
Burn a Candle	To light a flame on a wax-bound wick
Burp	Oral, audible release of gas, usually referring to a smaller sound than that of a "belch"
Buy Clothes	While referring specifically to the exchange of money for attire, the act of buying clothes could also include choosing them, trying them on, and building ensembles
Call a Different Area Code	Dial a number other than one for which your own phone number shares a regionally designated three-digit code; now that people tend to keep their cell phone numbers as they move, "area codes" don't always refer to a specific regional area

Call a Friend	Dialing a phone for somebody with whom you have a relationship; many contemporary game shows use "Phone a Friend" or "Call a Friend" as an option to help find an answer
Call a Parent	Dialing a phone for a mother or father
Call a Sibling	Dialing a phone for a brother or sister; possibly including people who are not blood-related "siblings," but are siblings by way of shared communities
Call Home	Dialing a phone to reach one's current living residence
Carry a Purse	Usually while out of one's home or office, hanging a strapped wallet, sometimes with additional pockets, around a shoulder
Change a Light bulb	Typically after removing a burnt out or broken light bulb, screwing a new one into the socket; also the basis for countless old jokes (in bad form)
Change Clothes	Removing one outfit in favor of another
Check Email	Through a computer or electronic device, reading messages from friends and colleagues; it made snail mail an endangered species, but is being made a protective species, itself, by texting
Check Facebook	Through a computer or electronic device, reading messages from friends and colleagues, as well as reviewing a feed of updates, news stories, advertisements, cat videos, and other social media content
Check for a Bump	Check someone or yourself for swelling (e..g, when you bump your head or get a bug bite); in the case of pregnancy, checking for a BABY bump
Check the Time	Used to be done by looking at hands on a watch worn on one's wrist; today, it's usually done by looking at digital numbers on a phone
Check the Weather	There's an app for that, too; rain, shine, sleet, or snow discovered live or as it will happen; many find great pleasure watching whole channels dedicated to these natural occurrences
Check Voicemail	Almost as obsolete as snail mail, this is that form of communication where a person leaves a real, live, humanly-voiced message in your digital inbox
Cheer	A typically female's dance-like sport done with pom-poms to encourage teams toward winning a sport; also to cry out in happiness or excitement
Chew Gum	Close your mouth. Please.
Chuckle	Laugh – heartily – and sincerely
Clap	Two hands pushed together repeatedly to create a slapping sound that, when combined with other people's claps, makes a thunderous praise
Clean	Not dirty or disorganize
Clean a Closet	Make a closet not dirty or disorganized
Clean the Bathroom	Make a bathroom not dirty or disorganized
Clean the Microwave	Make a microwave not dirty, or, um . . . disorganized??

Clean the Oven	Make an oven (that's the inside, baking part) not dirty. Or forget it . . . just burn that crud off!
Clean the Stove	Make a stove (that's the outside, cooking part) not dirty
Clench Your Fists	To make tight hands with fingers and thumbs pressed together, usually in an effort to punch (or hold back from punching) someone or something
Close Your Eyes	Droop your lids over your eyeballs until you can't see
Clothes Shopping	See "Buy Clothes"
Clown Around	Means having fun and goofing off even though, for many people, clowns are not fun or goofy at all . . . thanks for that, Stephen King!
Color	What we see. Everywhere. Even if it's black or white or gray because those are colors, too! Okay, technically it's the light reflecting off of different surfaces in different ways making our eyes interpret different things that we call . . . yep . . . color
Complain	Much easier to do than to actually fix something
Complement Someone	To be somebody's counter-part, balanced match, or accompaniment (Did you think I would say to give somebody praise? That would be complIment!)
Compliment Yourself	To pay yourself praise . . . yep; compliment . . . with an "I"
Contemplate Life	Usually at a turning point, on the brink of a major life decision, or on the heels of great triumph or tragedy, consider the direction of one's existence
Contemplate Love	Decide, through thoughtful consideration, your emotional feelings for another person, either specifically or in theory
Correct Someone	What I WILL DO if you type "your" instead of "you're"!
Correct Yourself	Hopefully with humility admit being incorrect about someone or something
Cough	The inevitable bark-like sound to escape as a result of a tickle in one's throat; the urge that comes in the middle of the quietest point in the movie
Count	Dracula! Von Count! Of Monte Cristo! Unless you just mean numerically keeping track of and ordering things
Count to Ten	Okay, this really is just numerically ordering things, but only as many as you can keep track of on your fingers . . . unless you were born with fewer than ten digits on your hands or you lost one in an accident . . . OR if you have six fingers on your right hand, which could make you COUNT Tyrone Rugen from *"The Princess Bride"*
Crack a Knuckle	Don't. Not by pushing, pulling or twisting. Just don't.
Crack Your Back	Really don't. Have you seen people contort themselves? Ouch.
Crack Your Neck	Seriously. Don't. This one is the worst of all! Leave it to a licensed, educated professional!
Crave Junk Food	Desire to eat something that has low nutritional value and usually high fat, sugar, salt, or some other empty filler (but it usually tastes good especially after a heartbreak)

Crave Something Weird	To desire eating an individual food or a food combination that traditionally is not eaten or not eaten together such as pickles and ice cream, peanut butter and cheese, or crickets
Criticize Someone	The opposite of complimenting somebody; offering negative commentary, usually without a constructive suggestion for positive change
Critique Something	To offer an opinion and/or rating, usually negative, but possibly positive, typically for a work of art or performance and with intermixed suggestions for changes or improvements
Cross the Street	Look both ways, first!
Cross Your Fingers	"Hope to die. Stick a needle in my eye." Or, wait a minute. That's for "cross my heart." What an awful little rhyme. Good thing this one is more like wishing really hard for something
Cross Your Legs	Common way to sit in a chair, putting one leg over another
Cry	In the case of extreme emotions of happiness, sadness, or triumph, an involuntary leaking from the eyes, sometimes accompanied by a running nose, tight throat, an inability to make sounds other than vocal sobs
Curse	A witch's spell . . . or what you say when you stub your toe
Cuss	Definitely what you say when you stub your toe
Cut Fingernails	Intentional shortening or shaping of the nails on one's fingers
Cut Toenails	Intentional shortening or shaping of the nails on one's toes
Dance	To move in a rhythmic manner
Daydream	To allow your mind to wander, usually onto positive thoughts and imaginings
Delegate	As a verb, it means to pass along responsibility for a task; as a noun, this is a person who holds the power to elect government leaders in a representative republic (which is what the United States really is)
Deposit a Check	To sign a piece of paper and bring it to your bank in order to turn it into real money
Dine In	Eating . . . inside, or at home
Dine Out	Eating . . . out of the home
Do Mental Math	Usually using the basic functions of adding, subtracting, multiplying and dividing, figuring out an arithmetic problem based on the facts you know
Donate Food	To provide usually non-perishable edible items to shelters, churches, families, and foundations, typically to help those less fortunate
Donate Money	To provide financial resources to shelters, churches, families, foundations, and non-profit organizations, typically to help those less fortunate, but also with the purpose of helping raise funds and awareness for specific causes such as illnesses, storm recoveries, tragedies, and atrocities

Donate Something	Provide an item that is either specifically requested or is something you no longer need or use to an individual or organization that will make better use of the "thing"
Donate Time	The most precious of resources, this is to give of one's own, available hours to aid a person, organization, or cause
Doodle	When you do it in your notebook? Cute & quirky! When your dog does it on your floor? Definitely not cute & quirky.
Draw a Portrait	Drawing indicates simple lines and a portrait usually refers specifically to a human's face
Dream	Whether asleep or awake, imagining great things
Dress Down	For clothing this refers to casual attire, but – in casual OR formal attire, one can dress another down by speaking to him or her in a reprimanding manner
Dress Up	To wear one's "Sunday Best", or fancy or formal attire
Drink Coffee	Yes please.
Drink Juice	To swallow the squeezed, sweet goodness of various fruits and, sometimes—oh so sneakily—vegetables
Drink Soda	Swallowing the bubbly, colored, corn-syrupy, canned beverages most popular at large gatherings and summer picnics
Drink Tea	Swallowing a liquid (hot or cold) created from soaking (steeping) fragrant, spiced leaves and flowers; or, it can come as black dust in a paper filter bag . . . but why?
Drink Water	What we really should be swallowing as a beverage of choice for at least half of our bodyweight in ounces every single day; (if you weigh 130 lbs., you should drink 65 oz. of water daily)
Drive	To operate a vehicle OR to push your way toward something with positive motivation
Drop Something	Maybe you just let something slip out of your hand and it fell to the nearest surface, but you could also "let go" of a responsibility, obligation, or task
Drop Your Phone	Those phone face replacements? They don't work.
Drum Your Fingers	To tap one's fingers on a surface, usually in a rippling manner, creating a very light "drum" sound
Dust	Either the specks floating in the air and landing on surfaces (most of those are dead skin cells, by the way) or the act of removing said specks
Dust a Cobweb	You don't see the spiders, but you see those incessant webs . . . and they catch every bit of dust in the corners of your home
Eat	Take in calories
Eat a Cookie	Take in yummy calories
Eat a Fruit	Take in still yummy but slightly healthier calories
Eat a Salad	Take in the kind of calories you should take in if you're trying to lose weight.

Eat a Sandwich	Take in calories in the form of two pieces of bread around your choice of fillings from meat and cheese, to peanut butter an d jelly, to fried bologna and pickles
Eat a Snack	Take in calories you probably don't need, but they will fill you up until the next meal
Eat a Vegetable	Take in calories that were grown in the ground
Eat Breakfast	Take in calories first thing in the morning
Eat Candy	Take in calories on Halloween Night
Eat Chocolate	Take in calories made from cocoa beans, milk, and sugar
Eat Dessert	Take in sweet calories
Eat Ice Cream	Take in sweet, COLD calories
Eat Meat	Take in calories that were once living on the calories of things that were grown in the ground
Eat Off a Paper Plate	Take in calories using a recyclable cardboard contraption to display it and keep it contained
Eat Outside	Take in calories . . . take out yourself . . . whew . . .
Empathize	To feel sorry for somebody else, not out of pity, but because you have personally experienced what he or she is going through
Empty Trash	To take out the garbage, usually in one's home
Enforce a Rule	To remind persons of a policy, as well as the punishments should the policy not be followed; oh! Then ACTUALLY use the punishment if the policy is broken
Entertain	To create a joyful expression in others through music, dance, art, acting, reading, movies, humor, sports, circus acts, parades, or other positive experiences
Exercise	See "Aerobics" . . . but also any kind of physical activity for bettered health; also a specific act to better a specific life area such as; a vocabulary exercise to improve spelling
Exhale	The OUT part of breathing
Fart	Like a burp . . . except, from your butt, and often stinky, and just as often blamed on the dog
Feel Grass	Use the sense of touch to experience a lawn
Fib	A lie, but the word your grandmother used
Fill a Cup	To hold a drinking reservoir under a running faucet or pouring pitcher in order to add a beverage for consumption
Find a Penny	"Pick it up! All day long, you'll have good luck!"
Find Money	If it's more than a penny, still pick it up! Your luck is improving! (Oh, but if it's in a wallet, turn it in.)
Finish a Countdown	It takes Count Tyrone Rugen from ELEVEN using his hands
Flirt	To use body language, words, tone, and even attire to show romantic interest (casual or long-term) in another person; usually feels subtle . . . but doesn't look it
Fluff Your Pillow	To pull, tug, squish, and adjust one's bed adornment in order to create a softer, cooler, more comfortable head rest

Flush	When you do so in the northern hemisphere
Fly	Not the insect, but the act of traveling through the air, preferably in an aeroplane!
Fold Laundry	Hopefully when it's fresh out of the dryer, toasty warm, wrinkle-free, and smelling wonderful, flattening and gathering together the edges of clothing and linens to put them away into closets, dressers, and drawers.
Follow Instructions	To read, step-by-step printouts about how to do something or build something. These handy pamphlets are foreign to many husbands.
Forget Something	Leave behind an object that was needed.
Forgive	At that point Peter got up the nerve to ask, "Master, how many times do I forgive a brother or sister who hurts me? Seven?" Jesus replied, "Seven! Hardly. Try seventy times seven. *(Matthew 18:21-22 MSG)*
Fret	Don't do it! Unnecessary concern!
Frown	An upside down smile for an emotion upside down from happy.
Fuss	Worrying about something, in a frantic, busybody manner.
Garden	To grow things . . . in the ground . . . that actually turn a color other than the dirt of the ground.
Get a Hug	To receive an embrace. Better than war.
Get a Kiss	Also better than war. Done with the lips!
Get a Surprise	Experience the unexpected. Not good for 90th birthday parties.
Get Dressed	Put ones clothing on.
Get Massage	Yes please.
Get Scolded	To be yelled at . . . and probably followed by that upside down smile.
Get Sick	Catch a cold or the flu. Or, maybe watch another episode of "The Walking Dead" but on a full stomach.
Get Tickled	Physically, while annoying to have done, hilarious when you do it to your little children! Emotionally, this gets done in pink!
Giggle	Laugh, little and high!
Give a Fist Bump	Do you know that a number of bishops got permission to replace the "Peace Be With You" handshake with this during a particularly nasty flu season?
Give a Hug	Be the one handing out those embraces. Somebody in your life needs one.
Give a Kiss	You should probably have permission for this one if it's a first. On second thought, you'll just know. Sigh . . .
Give Directions	Don't do this in the seat next to your significant other while he or she drives. Or do. Just know that they won't like it! But, definitely do this to the friend on the phone who can't find your place!
Give Instructions	Providing the "How-To"
Glare	Stare with judging anger!

Go on a Date	To attend a meal or event with the purpose of getting to know one another and spend time with each other.
Go Outside	Leave. The. House. BREATHE.
Go to a Concert	Live music in public. Life is good.
Go to a Movie	Some things are best on the big screen. "Harry Potter", "Star Wars", and "Star Trek" to name a few. (Hey! I'm not playing favorites!)
Go to a Party	Depending on the setting this could be great or not so much. A celebratory gathering of people . . . so, I guess it depends on the people . . . and the particular celebration.
Go to Church	Attend a place of worship.
Go to Work	Head to an office or other place of business, although one could use the expression "go to work" without having to leave one's home premises.
Goof Off	Act in a silly manner, usually at an inappropriate time.
Gossip	To speak about others without them present, usually spreading negative messages.
Grieve	Privately mourn a loss.
Grin	Smile, with a sneakiness behind your eyes!
Grind Your Teeth	Most often a subconscious act, closing one's mouth and rubbing the teeth back and forth to the point that the actual teeth could become damaged.
Grocery Shop	To buy food, usually for one's home.
Grumble	To moan or complain.
Hang Laundry	Put clean, but damp, laundry on a line to dry. Today done really only for delicates and sweaters.
Have Fun	To enjoy oneself.
Have Sex	See "Have Fun" . . . and don't go checking this one off if it isn't true!
Help Someone	Emotionally, physically, or financially offer assistance to a person in need for any number of reasons.
Hiccup	Actually just done when the lungs and diaphragm are "resetting" for oxygen intake, usually from speaking, eating, or drinking too quickly. Poor Charles Osborne (1894-1991) began hiccupping at age twenty-eight and continued for sixty-eight years, right up until he passed away.
Hit Snooze	The slap, slide, wave, push we do to our phones when we realize we were way too ambitious when we set our alarm the night before.
Hold a Door	For a building or an elevator, prop open the entryway to allow somebody an easier exit or entry.
Hold Your Tongue	Abstaining from saying what is on your mind because it may cause more harm than good.
Hop	What bunnies do in fields and college kids do on bar strips.

Host a Party	This used to be about celebrating or spending time with friends and family, but today it usually means trying to sell a product (everything from Tupperware to candles to completely private items used in even more private places) through a home show.
Hug	Tightly squeeze with affection.
Imitate Someone	"Imitate someone." **"Stop it."** "Stop it." **"Mom!"** "Mom!" "Kevin keeps repeating me!" **"Kevin keeps repeating me!"** *(There are other ways too, of course!)*
Improvise	To make it up as you go. Great on stage, not so much in the work place.
Inhale	Take air in.
Interrupt Someone	Knock Knock. **Who's there?** An interrupting cow. **An interrupting co**—MOO!
Investigate	To look into something, usually something sinister or criminal, with the hope of finding answers.
Iron	To run a hot, triangular object over clothes to take out wrinkles and sharpen necessary creases.
Itch	Or scratch!
Jaywalk	To cross the street, but not where you should!
Jump	Kriss Kross, Van Halen, and Diana Ross can't all be wrong!
Keep a Secret	Not tell somebody's private news or background.
Keep Someone Waiting	Have somebody stalled out while expecting a phone call, an arrival, a departure, or a relationship.
Laugh	Giggle, but heartier!
Laugh at a Joke	What you did on "Interrupt Someone" above, right?
Laugh at Someone	Or, maybe what you're doing to me now for thinking that I thought you were "Laughing at a Joke".
Laugh at Yourself	It's okay. I know I'm a dork. I can take it.
Laundry	It can be the clothing itself, but as a happening, it can refer to the gathering, separating, washing, drying, folding, and even putting away of clothing.
Lead a Meeting	Be the person in charge of an agenda or the primary speaker or presenter during a gathering of professionals, volunteers, or individuals with a shared goal.
Learn Something New	Contrary to popular belief, this is something that old dogs CAN do!
Lick a Knife	Why?
Lick Your Fingers	Much better. Especially if it has frosting or, even better, cookie dough!
Lie	To tell a fib. OR to make your body horizontal. Oh past participles and English mix-ups, how I despise thee!
Listen to Music	Take in sounds that typically comprise songs.
Listen to the Radio	Take in songs or speakers interspersed with advertising and usually hosted by an on-air personality.
Lose at Something	To fail at a task or not win a game.

Lose Something	To not keep track of an object, usually your keys, and usually when you're already late to get out the door.
Lose Your Thought	To have imagined something and then, before getting to share it, no longer have it in your mind.
Love Someone	To feel genuine affection for another such that they are an important and intricate part of your life.
Love Yourself	You can't do the one above without having self-worth enough to do this one first.
Mail a Letter	To send correspondence through the postal service, UPS, or other carrier.
Make a Confession	To tell a priest (or, less formally, a trusted individual) about a personal wrong-doing.
Make a Correction	Fix an error.
Make a Face	It will stay that way!
Make a Mess	To dirty a place or a part of one's life.
Make a Mistake	To mess up.
Make a Promise	To tell somebody you will do something, say something, be true to something or someone, or go somewhere with the full intention of your heart to follow through.
Make a Sandwich	Put together two pieces of bread with any matter of nutritional content between the slices.
Make a Wish	A dream spoken aloud or to oneself, in the hopes that it will come true!
Make a Wrong Turn	To go the wrong direction, physically or metaphorically.
Make an Animal Noise	To use your human voice to create the sounds of dogs, cats, cows, coyotes, kookaburra birds, or any other manner of species that is not human.
Make Coffee	Yes please.
Make Dinner	Put together the final meal of the day.
Make Love	Do this instead of war.
Make Lunch	Put together a mid-day meal that gets taken to school or work.
Make Small Talk	To discuss any matter of relatively unimportant topics in an effort to pass time or relieve awkwardness.
Make Someone Else's Bed	Pull up covers and pillows on a mattress to create an attractive sleeping surface.
Make Something Up	See "Fib".
Make Tea	Yes please, but only if it's made with leaves and spices, not dust and powder.
Make Toast	Turn bread into a warm, crispy version of itself. OR, insert an "A" between "Make" and "Toast" and we're celebrating!
Make To-Do List	Jot down all of the things you need to accomplish in a specified time period or toward a specified larger task.
Make Whoopie	Not Goldberg. That would be "Whoopi". Not the pies, either. This is the singular (but shared!) "Whoopie" popularized by the 1970s game show, "The Newlywed Show". Don't kiss & tell!

Make Your Bed	See "Make Someone Else's Bed" and apply it to your own!
Make-Out	Kissing . . . and more.
Meditate	A combination of breathing and thinking to bring peace and direction.
Meet a Friend	Get together with somebody you like.
Meet Someone New	Often preceded by an introduction or a handshake, bringing an unknown person into your circle of acquaintances.
Mind Your Manners	Also "mind your Ps and Qs!" To behave according to proper etiquette.
Misbehave	Probably not minding your manners OR your Ps and Qs!
Miss Someone	To wish that a person not with you . . . *was*.
Miss Your Stop	To stay on a form of public transportation past the point at which you should have gotten off.
Moan	See "Grumble".
Mock	To make fun of somebody, often in a manner that is unrecognizable to the person him or herself. A form of imitation with exaggerated negative aspects.
Mop	To clean a floor with a wet application and a handled rag.
Mow the Lawn	To cut the grass in one's yard.
Nag	To repeatedly make the same requests to the point of annoyance.
Nap	To sleep, usually for a brief period of time up to an hour, and usually during non-traditional sleeping hours. Babies get to do it, though and it's awesome!
Negotiate	To discuss compromises until a shared conclusion is reached.
Nod	To use only one's head to indicate, "yes."
Paint	Put pigment on a canvas, a wall, or another artistic medium.
Pamper Yourself	To give yourself thoughtful or luxurious treatment
Pant	To breathe quickly and heavily as a dog after a walk or, in the case of a fat dog, after standing up
Park a Car	To put your vehicle along a street, into a lot, or on a multi-level or multi-tier structure for automobiles
Pass Gas	Fart; technically burp, too, but rarely used in that sense
Pay Bills	To send money to suppliers of home, insurance, electricity, water, medical services, vendors, etc., in order to ensure continuation of such service
Perform a Ritual	To act in a repeatable manner to achieve something routine
Pet Someone	Can be to stroke one's hair or clothing or to make out
Pet Something	Not the making out part . . . blekch!
Pick Your Nose	You can pick your nose; you can pick your friends; but you can't pick your friend's nose.
Pinch	Squeeze the skin, usually as a reminder or a wake-up; OR, to save money – specifically "pinch pennies"

Pity Yourself	To feel bad about your circumstance and sometimes to encourage others to extend the same sentiment
Plan Something	To make arrangements and organize an event, schedule, activity, or set of activities; Also to create a future vision
Play a Game	To engage in a set of rules over dice, cards, or boards with unique directions and in the attempt of achieving a pre-determined goal; Also, messing with another person's mind, usually over an emotional relationship or situation
Play an Instrument	To create music through a material item
Plot	To determine a path along a journey of any kind (storm, road, river, etc.)
Plug Your Ears	What you wish you could do nicely while at church and the person behind you is off by half a beat
Point	To direct attention by way of elongating the index finger
Post to Facebook	To put a picture, news clip, shared information, or status change up on your social media profile in order to allow others to read it
Praise God	He is good all the time. All the time, He is good.
Pray	*P* – (offer PRAISE for all that He's done in your life); *R* – (REPENT of any wrongs in your own life); *A* – (ASK for needs from God); *Y* – (YIELD to God's wisdom and will to have their way in your life). "AMEN"! (Which means "I believe!")
Prepare Breakfast	To cook, make, or set out the morning meal.
Prepare Dinner	To cook, make, or set out the evening meal, unless you live in the northeast or deep south of the United States, in which case "Dinner" means "Lunch" and "Supper" is "Dinner"
Prepare Lunch	To, cook, make, or set out the mid-day meal
Procrastinate	To put off something, generally of a negative nature, but why put off until tomorrow what you can do the day after that? (Wait. That's not right.)
Pull Weeds	To pretend that yanking a stray, unexpected, root-overtaking green from your garden will be gone forever when you remove it from the ground. It will be back. In a day or two. And stronger than ever.
Put on Jewelry	Adorning oneself with any number of items including,, but not limited to, rings, earrings, necklaces, bracelets, broaches/pins, headbands, anklets, toe rings, belly button rings (you know, if you still think it's 1990), eyebrow rings, nose rings, tongue rings, belts, or (for our friends in 1990), belly chains
Put on Make-up	For stage, it's thick, drastic, and colorful, like the mask of a streetwalker; but some base, lipstick, and mascara should be in every woman's purse (and a few guys, I guess, if you're into the whole guyliner thing)
Put on Shoes	SO MANY TO CHOOSE FROM . . . NEVER ENOUGH TO CHOOSE FROM!

Put on Socks	Do I have to?
Read	To peruse the written word for escape, fantasy, relatability, fascination, entertainment, information, joy, imagination, beauty, purpose, opinion, passion, insight, motivation, inspiration, planning, direction, vision, excitement, sentimentality, understanding, fulfillment, simplicity, complexity, intricacy, and the entire spectrum of human emotion . . . sigh . . .
Read a Book	See "Read" and put the words between two thick, sometimes leather, wooden, woven, or wrapped cardboard covers tightly bound as a beautiful bow around the conceptual creation
Read a Magazine	See "Read" and put the words between to glossy paper covers filled with photos, advertisements, and perfume samples
Read a Menu	Choose from a written selection of edibles at a menu
Read a Newspaper	See "Read" but, unfortunately, add shock, awe, negativity, judgmentalism from various angles, biased editorials and opinion pieces, and hopelessness – Then print it on some of the nicest smelling, thin, grainy paper that is ideal for folding or rolling; a dying print medium
Read Bible	He is good all the time. All the time, He is good. (In writing!)
Read Out Loud	To mumble or speak outwardly when perusing the words of any medium
Read the News	See "Read a Newspaper", but apply to any written news source from social media feeds, to websites, to smart device readers, and more
Receive Email	In an internet browser, obtain messages sent to a personalized electronic address
Receive Mail	In an actual box at your actual home, collect actual letters written in actual pen and pencil, on actual paper – NICE! Okay, but let's be real. The ACTUAL MAIL you're receiving is usually bills, advertisements, and recall notices!
Relax	To distress by any number of methods including, but not limited to laying down, meditating, reading, going on vacation, or sitting in quiet
Reminisce	To reflect back on something, sometime, or someone, usually with positive (albeit, occasionally, rose-colored) thoughts
Repair Something	To fix a broken item
Repeat Someone	To mimic, imitate, or say again the words of another person
Repeat Yourself	To say your words a second or third time to ensure you were heard and heard properly; rarely works with teenagers
Return a Call	Phone a person who phoned you first
Ride an Escalator	Take a trip up or down a moving stairway in order to ascend (or descend) a level in a building
Ride in an Elevator	Take a trip up or down a cable and pulley powered cart to rise or descend in a building, usually of three or more floors

Roll Your Eyes	The inescapable reaction that comes out through the eyes of a person (particularly of the teenage persuasion) when their most passive aggressive thoughts go through their heads
Rub Tummy	To pass a hand over one's abdominal area for comfort, fullness, nausea, or—in the case of expectant mothers—to say "Hello" and check on things with the tiny human inside of you
Run	Don't walk.
Run Errands	Not actually done running, for the most part, but rather done in a car going about town.
Run Late	To be on schedule to arrive late to an event, meeting, or appointment
Rush	To move quickly through a task or preparation of the task in order to accomplish it more quickly; can also apply to driving . . . or some pretty awesome drum solos of the metal era
Save Money	To live by a budget and decrease spending in order to increase available funds, usually for a future purpose
Say "Hello"	Greet
Say "Hi"	Greet, a little more casually
Say "I Love You"	The words you most want to hear from those you most wish to say it to
Say "I'm Sorry"	Apologize
Say "Thank You"	Express gratitude
Say "You're Welcome"	Acknowledge another person's gratitude toward you
Say a Prayer	Speak, either out loud or in your head, a hope, wish, or dream backed by the power of God
Say Your Name	"Laura Grebe"
Scold Someone	While often "yelling" at somebody, also can be pointing out a wrong or a fault at an average volume level; scold has a belittling tone, like that used from a parent to a young child rather than from a professional to his or her employee
Scowl	Furrow your brow in disapproval, like the face of Grumpy Cat
Scratch	Or itch!
Scream	Let out a shriek-like, high volume yell, often in frustration, but possibly in excitement or joy, as well
Scrub Floors	To thoroughly clean the "ground" of one's home, with a mop, brush, or rags
See a Play	Attend a live scripted performance
Send Email	In an internet browser, send messages to personalized, electronic addresses
Set Alarm Clock	Be honest. You use your phone.
Shake Hands	A professional hello, or a jazzy finish to a group dance!
Shake Head	The "No" of nods
Shake Your Butt	B-Double "O"-T-Y!
Shake Your Hips	Because they don't lie

Share a Secret	Tell a (hopefully) trusted person something that they may not know or expect about you
Shave	Remove hair from the body by running a sharp, thin razor across your skin (who started this trend, anyway?!)
Shop	Can be buying things you want for yourself or others or merely looking at them
Shop Online	Still perusing or buying things you want for yourself or others, but through websites rather than in physical store locations
Show Up Late	Arrive after an expected, scheduled time.
Shower	To allow water to run down one's body from an overhead faucet in order to energize, de-stress, or relax (see "Happenings in Time" later in this book!)
Sigh	To exhale with physical, mental, or emotional exhaustion
Sign Something	To write your name in a physical location
Sign Your Name	Hmmm . . . I wonder what else you *would* sign? Your "dream name" like you did in middle school friendship notebooks, perhaps?
Sign-In	To write your name down upon arrival at a (typically preregistered) event in order to make note of your attendance.
Sign-Up	To formally decide to attend a meeting, event, or activity by way of submitting your name to some sort of attendance list
Sin	To go against God in your thoughts or actions; the bad news is everybody does it; the good news is that you're already forgiven
Sing	Melodically form words and sounds
Sing in the Car	The place you will sound second best when melodically forming words and sounds
Sing in the Shower	Yep. You guessed it. This is where you sound best. Water acoustics rock!
Sit in Traffic	I wouldn't recommend actually *sitting* in traffic, but most of us do it in our cars
Sketch	To draw in a short-hand or haphazard manner, usually in pencil or in a single color
Skip	Half-jogging/Half-hopping
Slam a Door	Forcefully push a wooden closure shut
Slip	To nearly fall based on a foot sliding, usually because of a missed step or something on the ground
Smell an Herb	To take in the scent of a fresh cooking green
Smell Something Gross	Like when you drive by the sewage treatment facility
Smell Something Nice	Take an extra breath
Smell the Flowers	Stop and . . .
Smile	Make an upside down frown
Smirk	A sneaky smile . . . with a little something extra up your sleeve
Snap	Push fingers and thumbs against one another until one clicks down to the pad of your palm to make a high-pitched beat.

29

Sneak	To think something, do something, or go somewhere, with ulterior motives or without revealing any or all of your thinking, doing or going activity
Sneeze	Part nose, part mouth, all tickle and goosebumps, releasing in everything from a tiny "SQUEAK!" to a bellowing "AHH-PHAUGH!"
Snort	What you say when you're not the mother.
Snuggle	To cuddle together affectionately, usually in warmth or cozy layers and blankets
Solve a Puzzle	Possibly a jigsaw picture cut into pieces as you place the final part of the picture, but also to work out a riddle or mystery from found clues
Speak a Different Language	To master (or at least fake well) a tongue from another country.
Spend Money	To dole out financial earnings toward purchase of all kinds
Spill Something	Don't cry over the milk!
Splash	To toss or slap against water causing it to spray or spread
Splurge	To spend somewhat frivolously on someone (possibly yourself) for an item you usually would not spend money (or at least as much money as you've opted for in this scenario)
Squint	To squeeze one's eyes nearly closed, in an effort to glare or merely just see better
Stand in the Shade	Outside, to seek shelter from hot or blinding lights under a tree or near a building; metaphorically, much like "stand in someone's shadow," it is to fall to the background in somebody else's existence, perhaps feeling as a comparative underperformer
Stand in the Sun	Antonymous with standing in the shade, one would seek light, heat, and—metaphorically—the spotlight
Start a Countdown	In looking forward to an activity or event that is a measurable amount of time away, begin counting backward to the moment
Start a Habit	Begin doing a new activity; usually "starting" a habit has a positive connotation; BREAK the habit of smoking and START the habit of exercising
Step in a Puddle	Either with playful intentionality or by accidental misstep, to dip one's foot into gathered water
Step in Mud	See "Step in a Puddle" except, the puddle is sludgy and dirty
Stretch	Reach and contort the body in manners which elongate and improve a muscle's feeling of relaxation, either before or after a workout, at the start or end of a day, or following an extended period of standing, sitting, or laying in a single position
Strike a Pose	There's nothing to it!
Stub Toe	Hate this. How is it we lose track of where our toes are in relation to other things at their level?

Study	Focused time in the research, education, and application of a specific subject matter area
Surprise Someone	See "Get a Surprise" and remember to keep this one on the shelf for Grandpa's birthday
Swat a Bug	To backhand away a flying nuisance
Swat a Fly	To backhand away a flying nuisance that likes to eat poop
Swear	See "Curse"; also can be used as a dramatic take on "promise." "I didn't do it! I swear!"
Sweat	Expelling salted droplets to cool the skin when working out, working hard, or—in my case when I was writing this list—just working at creating a tiny human
Sweep	It is *SO* much more fun to sweep an awards ceremony than a kitchen floor!
Swim	Dancing, horizontally, in a pool or lake . . . not *that* horizontal dance!
Swing	Let's go with flying through the air on a rubber rectangle or wooden plank attached to chains
Take a Bath	Clean oneself while sitting in the stuff you cleaned off of yourself
Take a Break	What Alexander Hamilton should have done when Angelica came to visit to help avoid that whole Reynolds Pamphlet situation. Lin Manuel Miranda, we are not worthy.
Take a Nap	See "Nap".
Take a Picture	To snap a photograph, these days usually with a phone more often than an actual camera
Take a Selfie	To be the sole focus of the picture you are taking; according to Psychology Today, selfies can lead to extreme narcissism . . . shocker
Take a Taxi	Or an Uber these days
Take a Test	You may have control over an academic exam, but if this is medical, see "Pray"
Take a Vitamin	Consume nutrients in pill form . . . not nearly as satisfying as the foods they come from
Take a Walk	Just put one foot in front of the other!
Take Notes	Listen. Reflect. Write. Add Insights.
Take Off Clothes	Often leads to "Have Fun" and the activity that follows it in the alphabetical happenings list
Take the Subway	A speeding, underground electric railroad that carries large numbers of people between popular destinations or commuter pick-up points; can also run above ground in many cities including Chicago where it's called the "El" for "elevated"
Take Your Time	Antonymous to "Rush"
Talk About Weather	While specifically referring to a discussion about meteorological occurrences, it's also a metaphor for "Small Talk"

Talk on Phone	Not-so-ancient precursor to texting
Talk to a Friend	Exchange words with somebody you care about
Talk to a Neighbor	Exchange words, often of a less personal nature, with those who live near you
Talk to Your Bump	Babies in the womb begin to hear, first your heartbeat, then your body sounds, and finally the outside world, at twenty-three weeks gestation
Talk To Yourself	Everybody does it, either to work through something, in practice, in fantasy, or with an absent mind
Teach Someone Something	Pass on knowledge to another person
Tease Someone	Can have a negative connotation meaning to pick on somebody, or a . . . well . . . different connotation. Check out what I mean in the "Characterizations" section
Tell a Joke	Spread a story in the homes of sharing humor or inducing laughter
Tell a Lie	Or, as grandma says, a "fib"
Tell a Story	And now, you have a great tool to help you . . . especially if it's in writing
Tell a Truth	Be honest and open with others
Tell Someone How You Feel	When it's positive feelings, the anxiety FOLLOWS as you are (or your character is) hopeful that the feelings are reciprocated, when it's negative feelings, anxiety PRECEDES the admission because of the awareness of entering a negative situation
Text a Friend	Through a series of characters and emojis or, sometimes, by speaking to your device directly, send a full message in a short format to a person with whom you feel close
Text a Parent	See "Text a Friend," but for Mum and Dad
Text Partner	Just don't go all "Anthony Weiner" (his name should have been our first clue)
Think Bad Thoughts	To have negative imaginings about somebody.
Think Dirty Thoughts	Not necessarily bad, by the way, if the thinking is about your significant other
Think Happy Thoughts	To optimistically focus your mind
Tickle Someone	Walk your fingers on little sides and little toes and little arms and little bellies to find big laughs on tiny humans
Tidy Up	Clean up the house on its surface by putting away clutter and "left things"
Tie Shoes	Pulling the strings of primarily athletic shoes into knots and bows in order to keep them snug around the feet
Tiptoe	While it can mean to walk on the tips of one's toes, it also could just be walking quietly
Touch Money	To hold cash; a 2014 UK study found that there were more common germs and bacteria on a single coin than on a regularly cleaned toilet

Trip	To stumble while walking, either on your own feet, or on something on the ground
Try a New Food	Expand your culinary horizons with unknown tastes and textures
Try on Clothes	Even worse when women are growing tiny humans
Try Something New	Take a chance at an untested hobby, activity, or event to see if you might have an interest (or simply to be with others who have an interest in the hobby, activity, or event)
Turn Off Lights	Flick a switch downwards for darkness
Turn On Lights	Flick a switch upwards and let there be light
Twiddle Thumbs	Technically, the act of spinning thumbs around one another, but also an expression for idly passing time
Unwind	To de-stress at the end of a day
Use a Computer	Is there somebody left in the world who doesn't do this? Yet we forget to have our characters sit in front of a screen. Two lessons here: 1 – Our characters need screens in their lives to be believable today, and 2 – Our own lives need fewer screens because obviously those happenings that most inspire and motivate us, to the point that we want to create stories around them, don't have screens at all!
Use a Credit Card	Does your character slide the card or insert it? Make sure you have your timeline right!
Use a Napkin	Cloth? Paper? Decorated with pineapples or pink flowers? Maybe a collection of fast food drive thru napkins made of that scratchy brown paper? Maybe no napkin for your character
Use Sign Language	To speak in a language presented through hand signs
Vacuum	Think about the physical exertion and the noise of pushing around the dirt and dust sucking floor and carpet cleaner
Visit a Different Zip Code	This usually is referring to an out-of-state location when, in reality, different zip codes may be as near as a few miles away
Visit a Friend	Drop in on a non-blood-related acquaintance
Visit a Parent	Drop in on Mum or Dad
Visit a Relative	Drop in a blood relation other than Mum or Dad
Wait for Someone	Pause to allow another person to join you at an event or activity
Walk	Don't run.
Walk Down Stairs	How many stairs does your character take at a time as they make their way down a level in a home or building?
Walk in the Crosswalk	How not to jaywalk
Walk in the Street	This one is probably jaywalking, though
Walk on a Sidewalk	Especially if your character is walking a dog, he or she is more than likely on the concrete pathway rather than in the street
Walk Up Stairs	Do you (or does your character) take more or fewer steps when ascending levels as compared to descending levels in a home or building?

Wash Dishes	Soap, scrub, rinse, dry, put away and repeat constantly throughout the day
Wash Face	With a washcloth or by splashing?
Wash Hands	How often do you wash your hands? Now think about how often you've had a character wash his or her hands. Remember that each of these happenings brings our characters to life!
Wash Windows	This task, more than likely requiring the glass of one's windows to be pulled in (or down or pushed out), probably indicates weather, as well.
Watch a Commercial	Take in an advertisement on television or the internet
Watch a Movie	Take in a full-length feature
Watch a Sport	Take in an athletic competition
Watch the News	See "Read the News", except now there are pictures
Watch the Sunrise	The sun may rise in the East . . .
Watch the Sunset	. . . but it sets in the West. ~Owen Wilson, Shanghai Noon
Watch TV	Or, more likely, Netflix®, Hulu®, or Amazon Instant Video®
Water a Plant	Unless you have a brown thumb, in which case the plant dies
Wave	Move a hand back and forth in greeting or salutation
Wear a Coat	Put on an outer layer appropriate to the outdoor temperature and weather
Wear a Hat	While the hat could be for warmth, your character could also put on a hat to go catch a baseball game
Wear a Uniform	Put on usually unvarying (or barely varying) clothing items which designate one's job
Wear Flip-Flops	Once also called thongs, so if Grandpa tells you to put on a pair of thongs to go on a walk along the beach, grab the flip-flops
Wear Jewelry	See "Put on Jewelry"
Wear Pants	Put them on one leg at a time
Wear Pantyhose	Put on black, colored or nude-toned tights, usually with a skirt or dress
Wear Slippers	Bunny ones are warm and fluffy
Wear Sunglasses	Does your character need these all the time or just while driving?
Wear Your Fat Pants	Oh, come on! Don't pretend you don't have a pair of these! (It's okay. You probably have a pair of your "skinny" jeans, too . . . and I don't mean the ones worn by Millennial guitarists
Weep	Cry, usually quietly
Whine	Complain, usually about something petty or unimportant
Whisper	To speak in low, quiet, breathy tones so as not to be heard
Wiggle Toes	Move big and little toes around playfully or to warm up
Win at Something	To become champion of a competition, but one can also win at life or relationships through love and success
Window Shop	Looking at and possibly even holding, using, or trying on merchandise for the mere fun of experiencing the item, but not actually purchasing

Wink	To blink one eye, usually in a fun, playful, loving, or flirtatious manner
Wish	Thinking (or stating aloud) a hope or dream
Work	Any manner of activity done to accomplish a greater goal beyond oneself and usually for monetary compensation; however, volunteering (unpaid labor) is also "work"
Workout	Exercise, but the implication is that the exercise is done to exertion, sweat, and with the goal of gaining or maintaining one's physical health
Worry	To have concerns over events for which there are possible negative outcomes and over which you don't (or your character doesn't) typically have control
Worship	Any act done with Divine leading in the hope of bringing glory to God including, but not remotely limited to: singing, tithing, praying, speaking, studying, serving, working, and communicating
Write a Note	Drop a personal line to somebody, usually on real paper rather than by electronic means
Write in Colors	See "Sketch," "Take Notes," and "Write a Note" and add ROY G BIV!
Write in Pen	Place ink on a page
Write in Pencil	Place ~~lead~~ graphite on a page
Write the Date	In some order based on the way you were taught, jot down the current day, month, and year
Write Your Name	You could be signing something or simply jotting down your own moniker on a page or in a notebook
Yawn	Usually done as an action of exhaustion, the wide-mouthed, slow and deep swallow of air is highly contagious when viewed by others
Yoga	A series of meditative stretches good for balance, exercise, peace, and overall help
Zip a Zipper	Note this does not say you "zipper" a zipper or "zipper" something up!

Word

Word Play!

Play

Word Play!

Word

Play

Play

Word
Word Play!

WORD PLAY . . . YOUR Happenings Dictionary

I bet you're wishing you weren't such an overachiever in creating all of those extra words and phrases, now!

This is the part of the book when you create your own definitions for your own happenings list. Don't be ridiculous about it.

A cat is not a dog, for instance. You should still start out with those great, tried-and-true, time-tested dictionaries. Then, add your own flair and understanding to your happenings definitions.

Use the boxes below and on the next few pages to define some of the happenings you wrote down in your first word play. If you prefer, you could also add to the definitions created in the list of 500+ Happenings or come up with even MORE happenings of your own to put meanings to in the table, below.

WORD OR PHRASE	DEFINITION

WORD OR PHRASE	DEFINITION

WORD OR PHRASE	DEFINITION

The
Happenings
Thesaurus
The
Happenings
THESAURUS
Happenings
Thesaurus

The

"The Happenings Thesaurus"

So what happens when you have the idea for an action, but the wording still doesn't seem right? Like, you know in your head what your character is doing or what is happening to your character, but the traditional phrase you use in your own life doesn't quite encompass what is happening in relation to your character — or at least not in a way that thoroughly engages and entraps the reader as you the writer intends.

The following pages contain essentially a thesaurus for happenings. It's the list alphabetically-organized you read through (okay, glanced over because you're not really going to spend the time reading everything in detail this first go through, are you?) a moment ago, but with alternative wording suggestions.

I mean, the same activity — the same happening — can take completely different spins depending on how you word it or accent it. And as writers, we want to be exact. We want to be precise. We want to deliver an experience to the reader that is the experience we intend to deliver.

And like before, when we do hit it right, when we do find the words to create the experience we want, if we're lucky, we are totally freaking out with the amazeballs scenes we create!

So here's a thesaurus for 500+ happenings. Because mental math is fun, if there is an average of three synonymous phrases for each of the 500+ (okay, 503) happenings, that means what we really have here is a list of over 1,500 actions for your character. That's 1,509 to be exact. And for the heck of it, let's throw the antonyms in there as well. Assuming the average of at least two antonyms for each happening, that's another 500 words or phrases (okay, 503); that means you have over 2,000 words and phrases (yeah, yeah; I know; we're up to 2,012!) that you can use to build a strong character.

Heck, let's be real. There's actually an average of two antonymous phrases for each of the activities below. That's a grand total of at least 2,515 happenings that you could and should use to prove your character exists.

Sometimes, I came up with one, two, three, or even more synonyms or antonyms. Feel free to add in your own! Other times, I've left opportunities for you to build the list with your own synonyms or antonyms. You'll see a few of those in the list. I've asked "Your synonyms?" or "Your antonyms?"

I present to you the thesaurus of happenings according to an **Experimental Word Player**. That's still totally kinky.

WORD OR PHRASE	SYNONYMS (OR NOTES)	ANTONYMS (OR NOTES)
Accept a *Compliment*	Praise, Flattery, Kiss-up	Negativity, Criticism, Insult
Accept *Responsibility*	Ownership, Accountability, Charge	Abdication, Delegation
Aerobics	Exercise, Dance, Jazzercise	Couch Potato-ing (Sure, why not?)
Agonize	Worry	Forget
Answer a *Question*	Query, Request	Answer, Result
Apologize	Say Sorry	Forgive
Ask a *Question*	See "Question" Above	See "Question" Above
Ask *Directions*	Instructions, Steps	Haphazardly put together the crib without every reading the pamphlet and wondering why you have so many "extra parts"!
Ask for *Help*	Assistance, Leadership, Guidance, A Hand	Struggle, Go it alone
Attend a Meeting	Go to an Appointment, Go to a Gathering	Skip out, Stand up
Avoid an *Accident*	Swerve	Crash, Hit, Fender-Bender
Avoid Someone	Hide, Disappear	Run into someone, Acknowledge someone
Avoid Something	Do tasks other than those which are unpleasurable, Procrastinate	JUST DO IT!
Balance Checkbook	Checks & Balances, Debits & Credits	Overdraw, Bounce
Be *Brave*	Courage, Strength	Timidity, Cowardice
Be *Inappropriate*	Disrespectful, Unprofessional	Classy, Appropriate
Beep	Honk	Shhhhhhhh……..
Belch	Burp, Gas	Be Ladylike (Stereotypes are based in truths!)
Bite a Fingernail	Bite a nail	Manicure
Bite Your Lip	Chew Your Lips	I guess, NOT bite your lip? Suck your lip, Lick your lip
Bite Your Nails	Bite a fingernail	Manicure
Bite Your Tongue	Chew your food! NOT talk with food in your mouth.	Again, simply to NOT bite one's tongue –or, in the case of the metaphorical meaning, to "speak one's mind."
Blink	Shut eyes, Wink	Stare
Blow dry Hair	Heat-Dry Hair, Diffuse Hair	Air Dry
Blow Nose	Honk, Wipe	Let your nose run (eeww!)
Blush	Flush, Rose	To be pale, fair, or unchanged

Boil Water	Heat, Cook	Freeze Water
Bow	Bend, Curtsy, Handshake (Not really a synonym so much as a replacement)	Stand Tall
Break a Habit	Quit	Keep at a habit
Break a Nail	Break a fingernail, Break a toenail (specificity brings meaning)	Possibly to stub a toe . . . not an opposite, but a DIFFERENT result
Break a Promise	Lie, Fib, Cheat, Betray	Keep a promise, Build trust
Break a Shoe	Break a heel	Salvage your shoe, Avoid sidewalk cracks
Break Something	Damage something, Shatter something	Fix something, Mend something
Breathe	Sigh, Gasp, Inhale, Exhale, Take in air, Let air out, Suck, Blow, Pant	Hold your breath
Brush Hair	Comb hair, Pick hair	Dreadlocks, Rat's Nest, Tease
Brush Teeth	Clean teeth, Floss (it's in the family, anyway)	Have plaque buildup
Burn a Candle	Light a candle, Melt a candle	Blow/Snuff a candle out
Burp	Belch, gas	Hold in a burp, swallow
Buy Clothes	Shop, Try clothing on, Retail therapy	Pinch pennies, Use hand-me-downs
Call a Different Area Code	Call out-of-state/out-of-town	Call locally
Call a Friend	Phone a friend, Ring a friend up, Dial a friend	Hang up, Text, Email (Not opposites, exactly, but different acts entirely)
Call a Parent	(See "Call a Friend")	(See "Call a Friend")
Call a Sibling	(See "Call a Friend")	(See "Call a Friend")
Call Home	(See "Call a Friend")	(See "Call a Friend")
Carry a Purse	Carry a wallet	Just grab your keys!
Change a Light bulb	Change a bulb, Change a light, Fix a light/lamp	Blow a bulb, Burn a bulb out
Change Clothes	Freshen up, Dress, Change outfits	Day to Night-wear
Check Email	Check messages, Respond to email/messages	Stay offline, Set a vacation response
Check Facebook	Check your feed, Check statuses	Stay offline
Check for a Bump	Feel for a baby bump, Look for a bump/baby bump, Check for swelling (from injury or bug bite)	Wear loose clothes, apply ice or an antihistamine, ignore physical appearance, avoid mirrors, apply Benadryl ™, Ignore the itching and throbbing.

Check the Time	Check a watch, Check a clock, Check a phone	Let time slip away . . .
Check the Weather	Check the temperature	Leave the house for the day and just guess what to wear! Tank top in January!
Check Voicemail	Check messages	Ignore Messages
Cheer	Shout, Celebrate, Exclaim in excitement	Jeer, Boo
Chew Gum	Smack gum (blekch!)	Spit gum out
Chuckle	Laugh Heartily, Snicker	Be straight-faced, Not break
Clap	Applaud, Snap, Shuffle one's feet, Give a standing ovation	Be silent
Clean	Organize, Arrange, Dust, Vacuum, Wash	Make a mess
Clean a Closet	See "Clean"; also, Color coding	Shove stuff in there; that's what it's for!
Clean the Bathroom	See "Clean"; also, Changing the towels	What would be *your* opposite of a Clean the Bathroom?
Clean the Microwave	See "Clean"; also, Wiping down	Splatter the microwave
Clean the Oven	See "Clean"; also Self-clean/auto-clean	Burn it off
Clean the Stove	See "Clean"; also, Wiping down	Splatter the stovetop or range
Clench Your Fists	Make a fist; Ball up your hands	RELAX; Arms hanging
Close Your Eyes	Blink, Sleep, Possibly meditate	Open your eyes, Stare
Clothes Shopping	See "Buy Clothes"	See "Buy Clothes
Clown Around	Goof off, Mess around, Josh around	Straighten up, Behave, Follow the rules
Color	Add pigment (like aubergine!)	Remove pigment, Use whiteout, Erase
Complain	Grumble, Moan, Point out fault	Praise, Brag, Recommend
***Complement* Someone**	Partner/Collaborate/Join/Match with someone	Be polar opposites, Clash
Compliment Yourself	Self-praise, Esteem, Confidence	Put yourself down, Negative self-talk
***Contemplate* Life**	Think, Consider, Imagine, Dream, Reconsider direction	Drift, Default existence
Contemplate Love	See "Contemplate Life" and apply the thought process to love and affection	Fall head over heels, Be gaga (not the Lady, but Gaga in love, which can actually turn you into a little monster!)

Correct Someone	Fix grammar, Point out mistakes	Allow mistakes to slip, Ignore wrongs
Correct Yourself	Change direction positively; Fix one's one misspeaking	Be prideful
Cough	Expel mucus (blekch), Hack, Choke	Clear lungs, Breathe, Chew
Count	Numerically order	Possibly count *down*!
Count to Ten	Count your fingers, Count your toes, Take a breath, Calm down (the latter two dependent upon context)	Act immediately
***Crack* a Knuckle**	Pull, Twist, Pop (a finger or knuckle)	Elegant, prim, and proper posture, mannerisms, and tics would be antonymous with bone-cracking of any kind for you or your characters, Be stiff, Don't stretch
***Crack* Your Back**	Pull, Twist, Pop (your back)	
***Crack* Your Neck**	Pull, Twist, Pop (your neck or head)	
Crave *Junk Food*	Salty snacks, Sugar, Fat, Crap	Eat healthy
Crave Something Weird	Hormonal eating, Getting your freak on	Stick with the status quo
Criticize Someone	Put someone down, Insult	Praise, Compliment
Critique Something	Put someTHING down, Insult, Provide feedback	Praise, Compliment
Cross the Street	Jaywalk, Use the crosswalk	Walk the line
Cross Your Fingers	Wish, Hope	Go on faith
Cross Your *Legs*	Ankles, Knees	Straddle
Cry	Sob, Break down, Whimper, Blubber, Wail, Bawl, Shed tears	Laugh, Giggle, Guffaw, Chuckle, Snicker
Curse	Swear, Scream, Push against	Welcome, Invite, Praise
Cuss	Use foul language	Speak properly
***Cut* Fingernails**	Snip, Trim, Shape, File, Manicure	Chew nails, Grow nails, Break nails
Cut Toenails	Snip, Trim, Shape, File, Pedicure	Grow nails, Break nails
Dance	Move, Sway, Rock out, Feel the beat	Be still, Be sedentary
Daydream	Allow the mind to drift, Imagine, Picture, Envision	Be realistic
Delegate	Assign, Share, Collaborate	Take ownership
Deposit a *Check*	Money, A paid bill	Deposit CASH, Withdraw
Dine *In*	At home, At a friend's, At a familiar location	Go out to eat

Dine *Out*	In a restaurant, At an event	Eating IN
Do Mental Math	Figure, Calculate	Use Calculator, Guess
Donate Food	Give consumables	Take
Donate Money	Give financial assistance	Take
Donate Something	Give material gifts	Take
Donate Time	Give of one's limited availability	Not free your calendar for service
Doodle	Draw, Scribble, Trace	Take notes
Draw a *Portrait*	Picture, Painting, Person	Take a photo
Dream	In sleep . . . see "Daydream"	Quiet sleep, Forget dreams
Dress Down	Dress casually	Dress up
Dress Up	Dress formally or professionally	Dress down
Drink Coffee	Drink = Sip, Gulp; Coffee = the REAL "black-gold"!	Decaf, Instant, Sanka
Drink Juice	Specificity: Apple, Grape, Cranberry, Orange, Carrot, Tomato, Clamato (blekch!)	Inhale
Drink Soda	Specificity: Cola, White soda, Cream soda, Root beer, orange soda	Let it sit
Drink Tea	Specificity: Earl Grey, Chai, Herbal, Black, Chamomile, Oolong, Green, Red, White	Let it cool
Drink *Water*	H2O, Liquid ice, Solid steam, The living blood, Hydrate	Dehydrate
Drive	Conduct, Lead, Steer	Be a passenger
Drop Something	Let go of something	Pick something up
Drop Your Phone	Smash, Break, Lose	Pick up
Drum Your Fingers	Tap, Play, Beat	Be still, Fold your hands
Dust	Wipe, Clean	Dirty
Dust a Cobweb	Sweep, Catch, Clean	Let the spider live; Grandma always said, "Let one go to eat the bugs in the house!"
Eat	Feed, Intake, Nourish, Devour, Indulge in	Starve
Eat a Cookie	See "Eat"; add specificity: chocolate chip, oatmeal raisin, double fudge, peanut butter, etc.	Eat healthy, Eat a cracker
Eat a Fruit	See "Eat"; add specificity: banana, apple, orange, pear, mango, watermelon, grape, strawberry, raspberry, cherry, blueberry	Eat a cookie, Eat a salty snack, Eat a vegetable

Eat a Salad	See "Eat"; add specificity: potato salad, pasta salad, green salad, taco salad, chicken salad, tuna salad . . .	Eat a dessert
Eat a Sandwich	See "Eat"; add specificity: peanut butter and jelly, cheese, tuna, etc.	Soup is a companion, but could be used antonymously in the case of a meal that includes both
Eat a Snack	See "Eat"; add specificity: cracker, cookie, treat, popcorn, chips, etc.	Eat a meal
Eat a Vegetable	See "Eat"; add specificity: carrot, piece of celery, green beans, cucumber, spinach, radish, squash . . .	Eat a dessert
Eat *Breakfast*	The morning meal	Lunch, Dinner, Supper
Eat Candy	See "Eat"; add specificity: carrot, piece of celery, green beans, cucumber, spinach, radish, squash . . .	Eat staples or substance foods
Eat Chocolate	See "Eat"; add specificity: dark chocolate, milk chocolate, chocolate bar, chocolate truffle, chocolate cake, chocolate fondue . . .	Eat staples or substance foods
Eat Dessert	See "Eat"; add specificity: cake, pie, candy, ice cream, truffle, crumble, sweet bread, kringle . . .	Eat staples or substance foods
Eat Ice Cream	See "Eat"; define "type" of ice cream; is it actually: frozen yogurt, custard, gelato, sorbet, sherbet, iced milk, malt . . .	Eat staples or substance foods
Eat Meat	See "Eat"; add specificity: beef, chicken, pork, fish (it is the meat of an animal), venison, bacon, bacon, bacon, bacon, bacon . . .	Eat a salad
Eat Off a Paper Plate	Less dishes; more time with friends and family	Eat off the fine china
Eat Outside	Like "Dine Out", but more casual. More likely somebody's patio than a restaurant	Eat Inside
Empathize	Sympathize, Feel Bad, Relate	Misunderstand

47

Empty *Trash*	Take out the garbage/refuse	Let it pile up
Enforce a Rule	Carry out, Dictate	Ignore
Entertain	Perform, Gratify	Bore, Annoy, Exhaust
Exercise	Work out, Aerobics, Lift weights, (any specific exercise)	Be a couch potato
Exhale	Breathe out, Blow	Inhale, Breathe in, Suck
Fart	Pass gas, Break wind, Cut the cheese, Rip one out, Squeak one out, Toot	Hold it in . . .
Feel Grass	Toes in the grass, Touch the lawn	Your antonyms?
Fib	Lie, Be dishonest	Tell the truth, Be honest
Fill a Cup	Pour into a cup	Empty a cup
Find a Penny	Find a coin, Find luck	Miss a penny
Find Money	Locate/Discover/Come upon . . . Dollar/Coin/Moolah . . .	Lose money, Lose it all, Drop money
Finish a Countdown	Complete something, Arrive at a date/time/event	Start a countdown
Flirt	Tease, Lean in	Be "stand-offish", Give off an "unavailable" vibe
Fluff Your Pillow	Shape, Form	Punch, Flatten
Flush	Blush, Redden	Pale
Fly	Soar, Glide through the air	Run, Walk, Crash, Submit to gravity
Fold Laundry	Do laundry, Fold clothes	Live out of the basket
Follow *Instructions*	Follow directions/steps/a guide, Obey orders	Do whatever you want
Forget Something	"I do not recollect."	Remember, Keep track
Forgive	Give grace, Give mercy	Apologize, Say sorry OR Be stubborn (*about* forgiving), Be unforgiving
Fret	Worry, Concern, Pace	Be calm
Frown	Pout	Smile
Fuss	Flap, Bustle, Bother	Ease, Rest
Garden	Plant, Tend, Weed, Grow	Kill (plants), Dehydrate, Buy (rather than grow)
Get a *Hug*	Embrace, Squeeze	Handshake (Ouch! Rough date finish!)
Get a *Kiss*	Peck, Smooch, Sugar, French, Mwah!	Handshake (Yep! Still sucks.)
Get a *Surprise*	Shock, Unexpected pleasure	As expected
Get Dressed	Clothe, Change	Disrobe, Strip down, (also) Change
Get Massage	Rub down	Get tense

Get Scolded	Yelled at, Screamed at, Reprimanded	Praised, Complimented
Get Sick	Get ill, Catch something, Get a bug, Come down with something	Stay healthy, Feel well
Get Tickled	Poked	Not be ticklish, Get annoyed
Giggle	Laugh, Chuckle, Guffaw	Cry, Sob, Wail, Whimper
Give a Fist Bump	Exploding fist, "Hit me!"	Handshake
Give a Hug	Embrace, Squeeze	Handshake (Ouch! Rough date finish!)
Give a Kiss	Peck, Smooch, Sugar, French, Mwah!	Handshake (Yep! Still sucks.)
Give *Directions*	Give Distance/Landmarks/ Turns	"Move along, now."
Give Instructions	Steps, Guidance, Direction	Questions
Glare	Stare, Glower	Blink
Go on a Date	Go out, Step out	Stay in
Go Outside	Exit, Leave, Head out	Stay in, Hermit in
Go to a *Concert*	Band, Performance, Music Presentation	Lecture, Speaker
Go to a Movie	Film, Flick, Feature, Blockbuster	Television show, Play
Go to a Party	Gathering, Night out	Stay in, Go out alone
Go to Church	Go worship, Celebrate God	Worship alone, Go to work
Go to *Work*	The job, The office	Call in sick
Goof Off	Clown around, Josh around, Misbehave	Follow the rules, Behave, Stay in line
Gossip	Chatter, Talk behind people's backs	Keep secrets, Use discretion, Share positivity
Grieve	Mourn, Honor loss	Celebrate, Meet
Grin	Smile	Frown
Grind Your Teeth	Rub, Slide	Where a mouth guard
Grocery Shop	Shop, Pick up food	Order in, Go out
Grumble	Moan, Complain	Praise, Compliment, Be silent
Hang Laundry	Dry laundry, Put laundry on the line	Machine dry
Have *Fun*	Enjoyment, Pleasure	Boredom, Displeasure
Have *Sex*	Whoopie, Make Love, Do the horizontal dance, Sleep together, And – in the language of middle schoolers - Do IT	Abstain, Cuddle
Help Someone	Assist, Give a hand	Block, Prevent
Hiccup	Hiccough (same, really)	NOT . . . you know . . . *hiccup*

Hit Snooze	Take 5/7/9, Slap the clock/phone	"Wakey, wakey, eggs and bac-y!"
Hold a Door	Get the door	Rude!
Hold Your Tongue	Bite your tongue, Hold back, Hold your peace	Speak out/up, Speak your mind
Hop	Jump, Skip, Bounce	Walk, March
Host a Party	Hold, Offer, Present	Be a guest
Hug	Embrace, Squeeze, Pat	Distance self
Imitate Someone	Copy, Repeat, Mimic, Mock	Be original!
Improvise	Make it up as you go/on the fly	Plan, Schedule, Organize, Structure
Inhale	Breathe in, Suck	Blow out, Breathe out, Exhale
Interrupt Someone	Cut somebody off	Allow someone to finish
Investigate	Study, Research, Look into, Question	Accept, Don't question
Iron	Press, Prepare Clothes, Crease	Wear wrinkles
Itch	Scratch	Soothe
Jaywalk	Cross against/into traffic	Use the crosswalk
Jump	Hop, Skip, Bounce	Walk, March
Keep a Secret	Keep Confidence	Gossip, Blab
Keep Someone Waiting	Hold someone up	Be prompt/on time
Laugh	Giggle, Guffaw	Cry, Sob, Wail, Whimper
Laugh at a *Joke*	Naming your baby "North West"	Naming your babies "Noah" and "Maddy"
Laugh at Someone	See "Laugh"	See "Laugh"
Laugh at Yourself	Be self-deprecating	Take yourself seriously
Laundry	Dirty clothes and linens, Clothing and linen at any point in the wash/dry/fold part of the laundry cycle	Do the sniff test
Lead a *Meeting*	Gathering, Appointment	Unexpected Visit
Learn Something New	Discover, Realize	Forget, Block
Lick a Knife	Sadism, Horror movie moment!	Just wash it!
Lick Your Fingers	Suck	Wipe off
Lie	Fib, Be Dishonest	Tell the truth, Be honest
Listen to Music	Songs, The radio, Pandora, etc.	Silence
Listen to the Radio	Talk radio, Songs, Sirius, etc.	Silence
Lose at Something	Fail	Win
Lose Something	Forget, Lose track of	Keep track of, Find
Lose Your Thought	Forget, Have on the tip of your tongue	Remember, Know, Recollect

Love Someone	Adore, Be fond of, Care for, Appreciate, Not "Like" but "Like-Like"	Hate somebody, Feel ambiguous
Love Yourself	Confidence	Self-loathe
Mail a *Letter*	Note, Message, Card	Email, Text
Make a Confession	Tell the truth, Admit something, Reveal something	Hold back the truth
Make a Correction	Fix	"Let it go! Let it go!"
Make a Face	Contort your face	Be still, RBF
Make a Mess	Dirty a place, Make a disaster	Clean up
Make a Mistake	Mess up, Foul up	Correct a mistake, Do something right
Make a *Promise*	Deal, Trust	Lie, Betray, Over-promise/under-deliver
Make a Sandwich	Sub, Wrap, Unwich	Soup?
Make a Wish	Dream, Hope, Prayer (though this is really more than a wish)	Bet
Make a Wrong Turn	Go the wrong way, Choose the wrong path	Go the right way, Follow directions
Make an Animal Noise	Moo, Quack, Oink, Woof, Meow, ROAR, Tweet, Squeak, Neigh . . .	Silence, Stillness, Language
Make *Coffee*	Java, Cappuccino, Espresso, Latte, Macchiato . . .	DECAF!
Make Dinner	Supper, A Meal	Breakfast
Make Love	See "Have Sex" . . . add emotion	Fight
Make Lunch	A Meal	Breakfast, Supper
Make Small Talk	Chat, Talk about the weather, Catch up	Awkward silence
Make Someone Else's Bed	Turn up a bed	Turn down a bed, Mess a bed
Make Something Up	Lie, Fib, Be dishonest, exaggerate, Tell a story	Nonfiction, Be truthful
Make Tea	Steep	Just water, I guess?
Make *Toast*	Crisped Bread	Bread
Make *To-Do List*	Task List	
Make Whoopi	See "Have Sex"	Sleep in the dog house, Abstain
Make Your Bed	See "Make Someone Else's Bed"	Turn down a bed, Mess a bed
Make-Out	Pet, Kiss	Cuddle, Abstain
Meditate	Stretch, Breathe, Be at peace	Shout, Be Chaotic, Panic

Meet a *Friend*	Acquaintance, Colleague	Stand up an acquaintance/ colleague
Meet Someone New	Make new friends	Keep your circles closed
Mind Your Manners	Be polite, Mind your Ps and Qs, Behave	Misbehave, Be impolite
Misbehave	See "Mind Your Manners"	Saving all my love for you!
Miss Someone	Long for, Yearn for	Disregard
Miss Your Stop	Overstay, Neglect	Get off
Moan	Grumble, Complain	Praise, Celebrate
Mock	See "Imitate Someone"	Imitation (POSITIVE)
Mop	Clean, Wipe	Dirty, Mess up
Mow the Lawn	Cut, Trim, Manicure	Grow
Nag	Harp, Beg	Be at ease
Nap	Sleep, Catnap	Stay awake, Keep going
Negotiate	Compromise, Coordinate	Give in
Nod	Shake your head "yes"	Shake your head
Paint	Decorate, Do art, Color walls (canvases, etc.)	Wallpaper! Ha!
Pamper Yourself	Care for, Indulge	Ignore, Neglect
Pant	Breathe, Huff	Hold breath
Park a Car	Find a parking spot	Double-Park, Walk, Bike
Pass Gas	See "Fart"	Hold it in
Pay Bills	Get specific: Pay the water, Pay the electric, Pay for internet, Pay the cable, Pay the mortgage, etc.	Overdraw, Go bankrupt
Perform a Ritual	Practice, Repeat, Have routine	Wing it
Pet Someone	Pat, Rub, Squeeze, OR, See "Make Out"	Ignore, Deny
Pet Something	Pat, Rub, Ruffle, or Squeeze	Ignore, Deny
Pick Your Nose	Dig for gold	Sniffles, Runniness
Pinch	Grab, Nip	Flick
Pity Yourself	Feel sorry for, Pout, Empathize	Be tough/resilient
Plan Something	Organize, Structure, Design	More winging it
Play a *Game*	Get specific: Board game, chess, Video game, Wii/PS/X-Box game, Battleship . . .	Watch TV
Play an Instrument	Get specific: Play the piano, Cello, Violin, Viola, Guitar (because it's hot), Saxophone, Trumpet . . .	Play the radio . . . another great "instrument" of choice
Plot	Plan, Set out, Determine	Wander (physically or metaphorically)

Plug Your Ears	Stop up, Block	Listen
Point	Direct	Nod Toward
Post to Facebook	Make a status update	Take a social media hiatus
Praise God	Worship, Give glory/thanks	Be prideful, Deny God
Pray	Appeal, Ask, Beseech	Lament
Prepare Breakfast	Cook/Set-out/Serve the morning meal	Order room service, Skip breakfast, Eat on-the-go, Be served
Prepare Dinner	Cook/Set-out/Serve the evening meal (or mid-day meal if living in the northeast or the deep south of the U.S.)	Go out to eat, Order in, Get takeout, Skip dinner, Be served
Prepare Lunch	Cook/Set-out/Serve the morning meal	Go out to eat, Order in, Get takeout, Skip lunch, Be served
Procrastinate	Wait, Delay, Put off	Be prompt/ahead of schedule
Pull Weeds	Futility in action	Grow a dandelion garden
Put on Jewelry	Accessorize	Go bare (ears, wrists, fingers, ankles, hair, and neck, that is)
Put on Make-up	Put on your face, Rouge, Powder your nose	Go natural!
Put on *Shoes*	Heels, Wedges, Flip-flops, Sandals, Boots, Booties, Taps, Character shoes, Dress shoes, Loafers, Birkenstocks, Sneakers . . . . (Never too many!)	Barefoot it! (You could be nude by the end of this page!)
Put on *Socks*	Argyles, Sport socks, Tights, Pantyhose, Thigh highs, Knee highs, no-shows, Ankle highs, Therapeutic, Fuzzy, Slipper socks, Wool socks, Cotton socks . . . (You need a lot of sock choices to go with all of those shoe choices!)	Still barefoot, bare-faced, and bare of accessories. You're ready for the beach!
Read	Peruse, Skim, Scan	Watch the movie, but the book is almost always better. Except with Cornelia Funk and Veronica Roth – better movies than books…and not counting fan fiction, either
Read a *Book*	Story, Tale, Fable, Nonfiction, Fiction	See above.
Read a *Magazine*	Periodical	See above.
Read a *Menu*	Food options	See above.

Read a *Newspaper*	Journal, Press, Paper	Read your feed
Read *Bible*	God's true word, The Gospel, The Book of (Genesis, Exodus, Mathew, Mark, Luke, John, Galatians, Philippians, and on and on for 66 books, or 70 if you're Catholic)	Go it alone
Read Out Loud	Perform, Narrate	Read silently in your head
Read the News	Read the paper	Watch the news
Receive *Email*	Mail, Online messages	Postal Delivery, Actual paper mail
Receive *Mail*	Letter, Postcard, Bill (let's be honest)	Email
Relax	Rest, Refresh, Rejuvenate	Panic
Reminisce	Remember, Be nostalgic	Forget, Move on
Repair Something	Fix, Mend	Break, Smash, Shatter, Destroy
Repeat Someone	Mimic, Mock, Imitate	Be original, Be silent
Repeat Yourself	Clarify, Enunciate (Reasons, but also as synonyms)	*(Didn't you hear me the first time?)*
Return a Call	Call back	Ignore, Hang up, Text
Ride an Escalator	The Moving Stairs	Take the stairs, Take the elevator
Ride in an Elevator	Lift	Take the stairs, Take the escalator
Roll Your Eyes	Be a teenager	Be sincere
Rub Tummy	Massage, Stretch	Let it all hang out
Run	Sprint, Flee	Walk, Drag your feet
Run Errands	Make stop-ins	Do it online!
Run Late	The synonyms we use: "Got a train," "Hit traffic," "Couldn't find parking" etc.	Be prompt/on time
Rush	Hurry, Hustle, Bustle	Take your time
Save Money	Budget	Spend
Say "Hello"	Greet, Acknowledge, Address, Meet	Say "Goodbye"
Say "Hi"	Greet, Acknowledge, Address, Meet . . . but a little more casually	Say "Bye," "Ba-bye," "See ya'!"
Say "I Love You"	Sorry, guys. No synonym for this one. If you mean, "I love you," don't try to get off with an "I adore you," or "I'm fond of you!"	Say, "I Hate You" Say . . . *nothing*

Say "I'm Sorry"	Apologize, Ask forgiveness	Refuse to admit wrongs
Say "Thank You"	Express appreciation	Say "You're welcome"
Say "You're Welcome"	It's nothing, No big	Say, "Thank You"
Say a Prayer	See "Pray"	Lament
Say Your Name	Introduce yourself	Be a wallflower
Scold Someone	Yell at, Scream at, Shout at, or Belittle someone (But please don't)	Discuss a situation
Scowl	Furrow your brown, Frown, Glare	Smile
Scratch	Itch	Soothe
Scream	Yell, Shout, Celebrate, Hoot, Holler, Whoop	Whisper, Discuss, Talk
Scrub Floors	Clean, Wipe, Mop	Dirty, Spill upon, Leave, Scuff, Mark up
See a *Play*	Production, Musical, Performance	Watch the movie, but if it wasn't already a book (see "Read"), the play is almost always better!
Send Email	See "Receive Email"	Send Mail
Set Alarm Clock	Be ambitious	Sleep in
Shake Hands	Make introductions, Greet	Hug (to a certain extent), Nod the "Hey Neighbor" hello
Shake Head	Say "No"	Nod
Shake Your *Butt*	Shake your BOOTY, Gluteus Maximus, Bottom, Rump, Backside, Asset, Posterior, Tuckus, Arse, Trunk, Jello Jigglers, Rump, Hamhocks, Buttocks, Tushy, Hind-Quarters, Honky-Tonk Badonkadonk . . .	Top
Shake Your Hips	Don't lie	March
Share a *Secret*	Reveal a Confidence	Keep a secret, Break a trust, Gossip,
Shave	Nair, Wax, Smooth	Go natural, Recognize the winter; respect the winter
Shop	Buy, Spend, Search	Save
Shop Online	Cybershop	Shop small, Go to a store (they are these structures of steel and stone filled with actual, usually very kind people who help you find objects you need in exchange for currency)

Show Up Late	Make an entrance, Be tardy	Be prompt, Be early, Be on time
Shower	Wash up	Take a bath (or don't clean up at all, I guess!)
Sigh	Exhale	Breathe in, Inhale
Sign Something	Write, Scribble	Skip, Ignore
Sign Your *Name*	Moniker, John Hancock	Maintain anonymity
Sign-In	Register	Sneak in
Sign-Up	Register, RSVP	Show unexpected
Sin	Misbehave, Misstep, Be human	Jesus Christ
Sing	Make music, Hum	Be silent
Sing in the *Car*	Automobile, Vehicle, Van, Motorcycle, Bike (of the Harley variety), OR, Add specificity: Ford, Dodge, Porsche, Jag . . .	Walking, Cycling
Sing in the Shower	Belt out	Listen to the water
Sit in Traffic	Stuck in traffic, Delayed in traffic, Stopped in traffic	Have a quick commute, Get every light (green), Make great time
Sketch	Draw, Scribble, Design	Erase
Skip	Hop, Jump, Bounce	Walk, March
Slam a Door	Wham/Bang/Crash that door!	Creak a door shut, Open a door
Slip	Fall, Trip, Let go	Be steady, Keep balance
Smell an Herb	Get specific: Basil, Oregano, Lemongrass, Mint, Parsley, Sage, Rosemary, and Thyme, (I tried – but it's impossible NOT to think of those four together!), and on . . .	Touch, See, Taste the Herb (although it would be hard to taste without the smell happening)
Smell Something Gross	Wrinkle your nose	Smell the roses
Smell Something Nice	Morning coffee, Bacon, Cinnamon, Christmas pine, Spring lilacs	Cover your nose
Smell the Flowers	Take your time (Going metaphorical, here!)	Hurry along oblivious to surroundings
Smile	Grin	Frown
Smirk	Sneaky or arrogant grin	RBF
Snap	Click	Clap
Sneak	Tiptoe, Slink	Bull in a china shop, or a dog in the cone of shame
Sneeze	Ah-ah-achoo!	Hold it in
Snort	Grunt	Squeak, Sniffle

Snuggle	Cuddle, Be close	A toddler . . . who has learned to walk . . . and discovered the Tupperware ® cabinet
Solve a Puzzle	Work/figure a puzzle	Get stumped
Speak a Different Language	Learn a new tongue, Be bilingual (trilingual/multilingual)	Monolinguistic
Spend *Money*	Cash, Moolah, Dough, Bread and Butter, Bacon, Cookies (Money & Food have a lot of the same words!) . . .	Be broke, Bankrupt, OR Save
Spill Something	Dump, Pour, Drop	Clean up, Wipe up, Carefully fill
Splash	Splish, Wave, Slap Water	Feel the current (of running water)
Splurge	Spend, Overspend, Indulge, Overindulge	Conserve, Pinch pennies
Squint	Wrinkle your eyes, Narrow your eyes	Stare wide-eyed
Stand in the *Shade*	Shadows, Darkness, Coolness	Sun, Light, Warmth, Brightness
Stand in the Sun	Light, Warmth, Brightness	Shade, shadows, darkness, coolness
Start a Countdown	Count backwards, Count toward something	Count up
Start a Habit	Begin, Commence, Initiate, Open	Break a habit, Quit
Step in a Puddle	Splash, Slosh, Jump	Avoid, Skip over, Jump ove
Step in *Mud*	Muck, Dirt, Grime	Clear water Clean water
Stretch	Exercise, Yoga, Pilates, Meditation	Slouch
Strike a Pose	VOGUE	Candid shot
Stub Toe	!@%$#@^&%^&($#@!&!	Walk
Study	Research, Work on, Look into, Develop, Consult	Wikipedia
Surprise Someone	Bring the unexpected	Who blew it?
Swat a Bug	Flick, Brush, Smack	Ignore, Capture
Swat a Fly	See above	See above
Swear	Cuss, Curse, Use foul language	Be prim and proper
Sweat	Exercise, Clear the pores	Deodorant/Antiperspirant
Sweep	Broom (Yes – some people use it as a verb; they're wrong; and your synonym?)	Vacuum, Mop

Swim	Wade, Dog paddle	Drown
Swing	Fly, Play	Throw, Slide
Take a Bath	Wash up, Bubble bath	Shower, Stay dirty
Take a Break	Take five/ten, Step away	Keep going, Nose to the grindstone
Take a Nap	Rest, Sleep	Stay awake, Keep going
Take a Picture	Snap/Capture a picture/ photo/shot	Be in the moment
Take a Selfie	Or just practice your duck lips	Take a groupie . . . wait. No. That's not right, either.
Take a Taxi	Uber, Rental Car, Limo service	Drive yourself, Take the subway
Take a *Test*	Exam, Evaluation, Trial	Slip through, Cheat, Copy
Take a Vitamin	Nourish	Eat your nutrients
Take a Walk	Go outside, Get a breather	Be sedentary
Take Notes	Write, Jot, Scribble, Outline	Memorize (or attempt to)
Take Off Clothes	Get naked (okay – it took a couple more pages, but we got there!)	Get dressed
Take the Subway	Take the El, Take public transportation	Take a taxi, Drive yourself, Walk, Bike
Take Your Time	Dawdle, Procrastinate	Hurry, Hustle, Bustle, Rush
Talk About Weather	Small talk, Chat (though you could ACTUALLY discuss meteorology)	Be real, Communicate
Talk on Phone	Call people	Text, Email
Talk to a Friend	Chat with friends	Text, Email
Talk to a Neighbor	Chat with neighbors	Text, Email, Ignore
Talk to Your Bump	Talk to your baby	Pretend he or she can't hear
Talk To Yourself	Think out loud	Your antonyms?
Teach Someone Something	Educate, Pass on	Hoard knowledge
Tease Someone	Flirt, Pick on, Poke at	Be serious and truthful
Tell a Joke	Be a comic, Be humorous, Work for laughs	Be serious and truthful
Tell a Lie	Fib, Be dishonest	Be serious and truthful
Tell a *Story*	Tale, Fable, Myth	Truth, nonfiction
Tell a Truth	Be honest	Lie, Fib, Be dishonest
Tell Someone How You Feel	Express emotions (negative and positive), Stand up for yourself	Deny/Ignore/Lie about feeings
Text a Friend	IM a friend, PM a friend, Message a friend	Email, Phone, Mail, Visit (in that order!) a friend
Text a Parent	See above . . . for Mum and Dad!	See above . . . for Mum and Dad!

Text Partner	See above . . . for your significant other!	See above . . . for your significant other!
Think *Bad* Thoughts	Negative, Mean, Unkind	Be positive
Think *Dirty* Thoughts	Filthy, Naughty	Clean, Proper
Think Happy Thoughts	Dream, Hope, Imagine	Dwell on negativity, Lament
Tickle Someone	Poke, Prod, Play with	Hurt, Hit
Tidy Up	Clean, Wipe up, Pick up	Mess up, Dirty
Tie Shoes	Tie your laces	Trip
Tiptoe	Sneak	Stomp
Touch Money	Hold money, Fondle money (not judging)	Just slide the card
Trip	Fall, Slip, Wipe out	Be steady, Be balanced
Try a New Food	Eat, Experiment	Order the same thing . . . every time
Try on Clothes	Put on clothes, Dress, Try outfits	Undress (AGAIN!?)
Try Something New	Do, Experiment	Do the same thing . . . every time
Turn Off Lights	Flick the switch, Shut down	Turn on the lights
Turn On Lights	Flick the switch, Flip on the lights	Turn off the lights, Shut down
Twiddle Thumbs	Fiddling, Drumming	Be still
Unwind	Relax, Rest, De-stress	Get wound up, Panic, Overreact
Use a Computer	Pretty much school, work, and life-required	Go off the grid
Use a Credit Card	Use Plastic	All cash all the time
Use a Napkin	Wipe your face/hands	Wiping your hands . . . on your pants
Use Sign Language	"Speak" ASL	Speak/Hear
Vacuum	Clean the floor	Sweep, Mop
Visit a Different Zip Code	Go out of state/town/country	Go next door
Visit a Friend	Drop in on a pal/friend/chum	Stay home and leave them alone!
Visit a Parent	See above . . . for Mum and Dad!	See above . . . for Mum and Dad!
Visit a Relative	See above . . . for a blood relation other than Mum and Dad!	See above . . . for a blood relation other than Mum and Dad!
Wait for Someone	Wait up, Hold on, Pause	Go, Leave, Abandon
Walk	Stroll, Meander	Jog, Run
Walk Down Stairs	Descend	Ascend, Go upstairs
Walk in the *Crosswalk*	Pedestrian walk	Jaywalk
Walk in the *Street*	Road, Avenue, Traffic	Sidewalk, Pathway
Walk on a *Sidewalk*	Pathway, Pedestrian walk	Street, Road, Traffic

Walk Up Stairs	Ascend	Descend, Go downstairs
Wash Dishes	Clean, Scrub, Wipe	Dirty, Pile up
Wash Face	Scrub, Cleanse	Yesterday's makeup . . . TODAY!
Wash Hands	Sanitize	Spread germs
Wash Windows	Scrub/Wipe/Clean windows	Spots and bird doo
Watch a Commercial	Watch an ad/advert	"SKIP AD"
Watch a Movie	Flick, Feature, Blockbuster	Television, Book, Magazine
Watch a Sport	Get specific: Football, Baseball, Basketball, Hockey, Soccer, Olympics, etc.	Watch a chick flick
Watch the News	Watch TV	Read the news
Watch the *Sunrise*	Watch daybreak	Sleep in
Watch the *Sunset*	Nightfall, Twilight, Dusk	Go to bed early . . . really early!
Watch *TV*	Boob tube, Idiot box	Movie, Book, Magazine
***Water* a Plant**	Feed, Hydrate	You're supposed to water them?
Wave	Greet, Wave down, Gesture	Ignore, hiding in your phone as if you can't see the person
Wear a *Coat*	Jacket, Parka, Fur	Freeze, aka teenage boys
Wear a *Hat*	Cap, Fedora, Sombrero	An updo
Wear a *Uniform*	Costume, Work clothes	Outfits, Wardrobe
Wear *Flip-Flops*	Thongs, Sandals	Go barefoot, Wear heels
Wear Jewelry	Accessorize	Go bare!
Wear *Pants*	Slacks, Jeans, Trousers	Skirt, Dress, Nudity
Wear *Pantyhose*	Tights, Thigh-highs	Bare legs . . . oooh
Wear Slippers	Fuzzy slippers, Bunny slippers	Wear socks or shoes, Go barefoot
Wear Sunglasses	Summer eyewear	Squint, especially when driving
Wear Your Fat Pants	Feel like crap	Skinny jeans day!
Weep	Cry, Whimper	Laugh, Giggle
Whine	Moan, Grumble	Praise, Celebrate
Whisper	Speak low	Yell, Shout, Scream, Ridicule
***Wiggle* Toes**	Roll toes, Flex toes, Wake up your foot/feet	Stand still
Win at Something	Triumph, Claim Victory, Score	Lose, Fail
Window Shop	Browse, Dream	Shop, Spend, Splurge
Wink	Blink	Roll eyes
Wish	Dream, Hope	Not imagine
Work	Go to a job/office, Labor	Laze
Workout	Exercise, Get healthy	Be sedentary, Give up
Worry	Be preoccupied	Let it go! Let it go!

Worship	Pray, Sing, Tithe, Give God the glory	Lament
Write a *Note*	Letter, Card, Message	Email, Text
Write in *Colors*	Get specific: Cattleya, Damask, Gamboge, you know – just the standard Crayola ® offerings	Black & White, Gray
Write in Pen	Ink	Pencil, Color
Write in Pencil	Graphite, Lead	Pen, Color
Write the Date	Month and day, MM/DD/YY	Vacation . . . who keeps track?
Write Your Name	Sign, Jot	Skip, Ignore, Leave blank
Yawn	Gape, Drowse	Caffeine
Yoga	Stretch, Meditate	Resting pose . . . that turns into just another nap
Zip a Zipper	What I am doing to this list before . . .	. . . opening it back up to help you use it!

Word
Word Play!
Play
Word Play!
Word
Play
Play

Word
Word Play!

WORD PLAY . . . YOUR Happenings Thesaurus

Your turn again! Just as with the Dictionary, let's not forget about YOUR Happenings. This is the part of the book when you create your own synonyms and antonyms for your own happenings list.

Here's where it can get really fun. Think about each of your phrases and try to imagine the happening in a positive, negative, or neutral light. For instance, if your character (or yourself in the case of a journal or other nonfiction, personal writing) "yelled", was that a yell across the house ("shouted for"), a yell in anger toward somebody ("screamed at"), or a yell of celebration ("whooped")?

Think also about hot, cold, and warm in relation to your word. For instance, and we'll work the antonym this time, the opposite of run: tip-toed (extreme/hot opposite), walked (neutral/warm opposite), and jogged (minor/cool opposite).

WORD OR PHRASE	SYNONYMS	ANTONYMS

WORD OR PHRASE	SYNONYMS	ANTONYMS

WORD OR PHRASE	SYNONYMS	ANTONYMS

The
Happenings
Categories

The
Happenings
CATEGORIES
Happenings
Categories

The

WORD PLAY . . . The Happenings Categories

"Your beliefs become your thoughts,
Your thoughts become your words,
Your words become your actions,
Your actions become your habits,
Your habits become your values,
Your values become your destiny."
~Mahatma Gandhi

I'm not pretending to have the profundity of one of the greatest peace activists in the modern history of man, but he was onto something that applies to this little Happenings experiment. Our existing is comprised of many levels of action. Sometimes those actions remain in our head or, in the most minor of ways, merely escape through our lips. At other times, those activities require physical movement, or, doing. Then there are those activities that require going.

What makes a character memorable? Usually it's not the physical description. It's the reader's attachment to or understanding of the character which can only be conveyed by the character's thoughts, actions and movements.

If the list of happenings is designed to be used to show characters exist (which, as the people who developed this list, we can guarantee that's the case), then these happenings must include happenings that show thinking, doing and going.

Happenings that occur primarily internally without physical action on the part of your character or someone else are grouped as "thinking" happenings. Happenings that are actions taken by your character are grouped as "doing" happenings. Happenings that are transporting your character from one spot to another are grouped as "going" happenings.

As you can imagine, some of these happenings fall into more than one category, and that's okay. Whether a happening is internalized by your character or positively acted out can further establish your character.

Depending on where you are, or where your character is, the manner in which you, he, or she exist could be limited to only the thinking category of happenings. A gut-driven character might spend a lot more time in the going list.

A faith-driven desperate thinker might PRAY, while a desperate doer could MAKE A PROMISE to God, and a desperate goer would GO TO CHURCH to seek community prayers and support. Or, imagine moving from AGONIZING over a mistake to APOLOGIZING for the wrong, to VISITING A FRIEND that needs to hear "I'm sorry" in person.

So without further ado, here, once again, is the list of happenings but this time divided into "thinkings," "doings," and "goings." Take a perusal.

Thinking

Accept a Compliment
Accept Responsibility
Agonize
Answer a Question
Apologize
Ask a Question
Ask Directions
Ask for Help
Avoid Something
Blush
Break a Habit
Break a Promise
Complain
Compliment Yourself
Contemplate Life
Contemplate Love
Correct Yourself
Crave Junk Food
Crave Something Weird
Criticize Someone
Critique Something
Cry
Cry
Curse
Cuss
Daydream
Daydream
Do Mental Math
Dream

Empathize
Flush
Forget Something
Forgive
Fret
Frown
Grieve
Hold Your Tongue
Keep a Secret
Lose Your Thought
Love Someone
Love Yourself
Meditate
Miss Someone
Pity Yourself
Pray
Procrastinate
Reminisce
Talk To Yourself
Talk to Yourself
Think Bad Thoughts
Think Dirty Thoughts
Think Happy Thoughts
Unwind
Weep
Wish
Worry
Worship
Yoga

Doing

1. Accept Responsibility
Answer a Question
Apologize
Ask a Question
Ask Directions
Ask for Help
Avoid Something
Blush
Break a Habit
Break a Promise
Complain
Compliment Yourself
Correct Yourself
Criticize Someone
Critique Something
Cry
Cry
Curse
Cuss
Flush
Forgive
Frown
Hold Your Tongue
Keep a Secret
Meditate
Pray
Procrastinate
Talk To Yourself
Talk to Yourself
Unwind
Weep
Wish
Worship
Yoga
Aerobics
Attend a Meeting
Avoid an Accident
Avoid Someone
Balance Checkbook
Be Brave
Be Inappropriate
Beep

Belch
Bite a Fingernail
Bite Your Lip
Bite Your Nails
Bite Your Tongue
Blink
Blow dry Hair
Blow Nose
Boil Water
Bow
Break a Nail
Break a Shoe
Break Something
Breathe
Brush Hair
Brush Teeth
Burn a Candle
Burp
Buy Clothes
Call a Different Area Code
Call a Friend
Call a Parent
Call a Sibling
Call Home
Carry a Purse
Change a Light bulb
Change Clothes
Check Email
Check Facebook
Check for a Bump
Check the Time
Check the Weather
Check Voicemail
Cheer
Cheer
Chew Gum
Chuckle
Clap
Clean
Clean a Closet
Clean the Bathroom

Clean the Microwave
Clean the Oven
Clean the Stove
Clench Your Fists
Close Your Eyes
Clothes Shopping
Clown Around
Color
Complement Someone
Correct Someone
Cough
Count
Count to Ten
Crack a Knuckle
Crack Your Back
Crack Your Neck
Cross the Street
Cross Your Fingers
Cross Your Legs
Cut Fingernails
Cut Toenails
Dance
Dance
Delegate
Deposit a Check
Dine In
Donate Food
Donate Money
Donate Something
Donate Time
Doodle
Draw a Portrait
Dress Down
Dress Up
Drink Coffee
Drink Juice
Drink Soda
Drink Tea
Drink Water
Drive
Drop Something
Drop Your Phone
Drum Your Fingers
Dust

Dust a Cobweb
Eat
Eat a Cookie
Eat a Fruit
Eat a Salad
Eat a Sandwich
Eat a Snack
Eat a Vegetable
Eat Breakfast
Eat Candy
Eat Chocolate
Eat Dessert
Eat Ice Cream
Eat Meat
Eat Off a Paper Plate
Eat Outside
Empty Trash
Enforce a Rule
Entertain
Exercise
Exhale
Fart
Feel Grass
Fib
Fill a Cup
Find a Penny
Find Money
Finish a Countdown
Flirt
Fluff Your Pillow
Fly
Fold Laundry
Follow Instructions
Fuss
Garden
Get a Hug
Get a Kiss
Get a Surprise
Get Dressed
Get Massage
Get Scolded
Get Sick
Get Tickled
Giggle

Give a Fist Bump	Lie
Give a Hug	Listen to Music
Give a Kiss	Listen to the Radio
Give Directions	Lose at Something
Give Instructions	Lose Something
Glare	Mail a Letter
Go on a Date	Make a Confession
Go Outside	Make a Correction
Goof Off	Make a Face
Gossip	Make a Mess
Grin	Make a Mistake
Grind Your Teeth	Make a Promise
Grocery Shop	Make a Sandwich
Grumble	Make a Wish
Hang Laundry	Make a Wrong Turn
Have Fun	Make an Animal Noise
Have Sex	Make Coffee
Help Someone	Make Dinner
Hiccup	Make Love
Hit Snooze	Make Lunch
Hold a Door	Make Small Talk
Hop	Make Someone Else's Bed
Host a Party	Make Something Up
Hug	Make Tea
Imitate Someone	Make Toast
Improvise	Make To-Do List
Inhale	Make Whoopi
Interrupt Someone	Make Your Bed
Investigate	Make-Out
Iron	Meet a Friend
Itch	Meet Someone New
Jaywalk	Mind Your Manners
Jump	Misbehave
Keep Someone Waiting	Miss Your Stop
Laugh	Moan
Laugh	Mock
Laugh at a Joke	Mop
Laugh at Someone	Mow the Lawn
Laugh at Yourself	Nag
Laundry	Nap
Lead a Meeting	Negotiate
Learn Something New	Nod
Lick a Knife	Paint
Lick Your Fingers	Paint

Pamper Yourself
Pant
Pant
Park a Car
Pass Gas
Pay Bills
Perform a Ritual
Pet Someone
Pet Something
Pick Your Nose
Pinch
Plan Something
Play a Game
Play an Instrument
Plot
Plug Your Ears
Point
Post to Facebook
Praise God
Prepare Breakfast
Prepare Dinner
Prepare Lunch
Pull Weeds
Put on Jewelry
Put on Make-up
Put on Shoes
Put on Socks
Read
Read a Book
Read a Magazine
Read a Menu
Read a Newspaper
Read Bible
Read Out Loud
Read the News
Receive Email
Receive Mail
Relax
Repair Something
Repeat Someone
Repeat Yourself
Return a Call
Ride an Escalator
Ride in an Elevator

Roll Your Eyes
Rub Tummy
Run
Run Errands
Run Late
Rush
Save Money
Say "Hello"
Say "Hi"
Say "I Love You"
Say "I'm Sorry"
Say "Thank You"
Say "You're Welcome"
Say a Prayer
Say Your Name
Scold Someone
Scowl
Scratch
Scream
Scrub Floors
See a Play
Send Email
Set Alarm Clock
Shake Hands
Shake Head
Shake Your Butt
Shake Your Hips
Share a Secret
Shave
Shop
Shop Online
Show Up Late
Shower
Sigh
Sign Something
Sign Your Name
Sign-In
Sign-Up
Sin
Sing
Sing in the Car
Sing in the Shower
Sit in Traffic
Sketch

Skip
Slam a Door
Slip
Smell an Herb
Smell Something Gross
Smell Something Nice
Smell the Flowers
Smile
Smirk
Snap
Snap
Sneak
Sneeze
Snort
Snuggle
Solve a Puzzle
Speak a Different Language
Spend Money
Spill Something
Splash
Splurge
Squint
Stand in the Shade
Stand in the Sun
Start a Countdown
Start a Habit
Step in a Puddle
Step in Mud
Stretch
Strike a Pose
Stub Toe
Study
Surprise Someone
Swat a Bug
Swat a Fly
Swear
Sweat
Sweep
Swim
Swing
Take a Bath
Take a Break
Take a Nap
Take a Picture

Take a Selfie
Take a Test
Take a Vitamin
Take Notes
Take Off Clothes
Take Your Time
Talk About Weather
Talk on Phone
Talk to a Friend
Talk to a Neighbor
Talk to Your Bump
Teach Someone Something
Tease Someone
Tell a Joke
Tell a Lie
Tell a Story
Tell a Truth
Tell Someone How You Feel
Text a Friend
Text a Parent
Text Partner
Tickle Someone
Tidy Up
Tie Shoes
Tiptoe
Touch Money
Trip
Try a New Food
Try on Clothes
Try Something New
Turn Off Lights
Turn On Lights
Twiddle Thumbs
Use a Computer
Use a Credit Card
Use a Napkin
Use Sign Language
Vacuum
Wait for Someone
Wash Dishes
Wash Face
Wash Hands
Wash Windows
Watch a Commercial

Watch a Movie
Watch a Sport
Watch the News
Watch the Sunrise
Watch the Sunset
Watch TV
Water a Plant
Wave
Wear a Coat
Wear a Hat
Wear a Uniform
Wear Flip-Flops
Wear Jewelry
Wear Pants
Wear Pantyhose
Wear Slippers
Wear Sunglasses

Wear Your Fat Pants
Whine
Whisper
Wiggle Toes
Win at Something
Wink
Work
Workout
Write a Note
Write in Colors
Write in Crayon
Write in Pen
Write in Pencil
Write the Date
Write Your Name
Yawn
Zip a Zipper

Going

Avoid Something
Attend a Meeting
Avoid an Accident
Avoid Someone
Buy Clothes
Clothes Shopping
Cross the Street
Deposit a Check
Donate Food
Drive
Eat Outside
Exercise
Find a Penny
Find Money
Fly
Go on a Date
Go Outside
Grocery Shop
Learn Something New
Mail a Letter
Meet a Friend
Meet Someone New
Ride an Escalator
Ride in an Elevator
Run
Run Errands
Run Late
Rush
See a Play

Shop
Show Up Late
Sit in Traffic
Skip
Spend Money
Step in a Puddle
Step in Mud
Swim
Dine Out
Go to a Concert
Go to a Movie
Go to a Party
Go to Church
Go to Work
Take a Taxi
Take a Walk
Take the Subway
Visit a Different Zip Code
Visit a Friend
Visit a Parent
Visit a Relative
Walk
Walk Down Stairs
Walk in the Crosswalk
Walk in the Street
Walk on a Sidewalk
Walk Up Stairs
Window Shop

Word
Word Play!
Play
Word Play!
Word
Play
Play

Word
WORD PLAY!

WORD PLAY . . . YOUR Happenings Categories

Your turn! Make a list of THINKING/DOING/GOING happenings based on your own Happenings list. Remember, some words may be on more than one list.

THINKING	DOING	GOING

Thinking	Doing	Going

Happenings

In

Time

Happenings

Happenings

In

Time

TIME

In

Happening in Time

So the 503 active phrases in these lists have been cataloged in a couple of ways so far. The list was even expanded to over 2,000 active phrases if the synonymous and antonymous phrases from the thesaurus section are included in this list. Without much work on your part, these active phrases can be further expanded to over 6,000 if the **context** of the activity is taken into consideration.

How many times have you walked your neighborhood? Dozens? Hundreds? Thousands maybe if you've lived in the same place all your life? How do you feel walking around your neighborhood in the morning — bright sunshine on your face, birds chirping, there may even be neighbors out starting their day? What about in the late day? Curtains closing in preparation of night, neighbors packing it in, the last laughs and happy screams as children are ushered in for bedtime rituals. What about in the middle of the night? Dark, quiet streets, with long, moving shadows cast from the occasional porch light, and the sounds of unseen animals moving across the lawns.

Not only can the time of day change the feel of these activities, but the time of day can change the entire meaning of an activity.

As writers, we want to harness all the meaning we can out of our characters' **happening**s. Choosing the right **happening** at the right time can further establish your characters' existence.

I'm a runner and I found that, whether I run in the morning, or at night, especially when I'm running outside, it really changes the emotion of what's going on.

Is it getting the blood flowing and refreshing me? Am I running out the stresses of the day? Or is it a little contemplative or even scary?

An example that everybody can relate to is SHOWER. When you take a shower in the MORNING, it wakes you up and rejuvenates you and you feel much better for facing the day. It's a great start.

Then, you take a shower at lunch after a workout, or at the END OF THE DAY, or before you go out at night, it's more about washing the dirt off from the day — getting rid of everything from the day and getting ready for something new.

Last, there's taking a shower at NIGHT and it's a completely different thing. It's more relaxing. It's distressing. You may even get the little massage thing on your showerhead pulsating. It calms you down and gets you ready for bed.

The same happening can have different feels for you . . . or, in your writing, for your characters. In the next **Experimental Play on Words**, enjoy a few thinking, doing, and going happenings broken up into short passages for various times of day.

Thinking

Check out these five thinking happenings done at different times of the day.

DAYDREAM

He sat like always with his coffee, toast and newspaper, but today he just started absently past the words on the page, daydreaming.

Tyler propped his head up with his arm and daydreamed out the window as his calculus teacher droned on.

He stopped with his hand over her doorbell. What if she didn't like him? A scenario ran through his head; one in which he was rejected, yet again. Before his vivid daydreaming came to an end, the door opened and he was face-to-face with the most beautiful woman he had ever seen.

Just an itty bitty experimental word play . . . how is DAYDREAM different at the different times of day? Go on. Play!

_____

_____

GRIEVE

She felt the warm sun but still could not bear to get out of bed. She was still grieving. It was still too soon. It will always be too soon.

He grieved. Why was the Earth still spinning when his life had stopped?

The house was asleep. With no one to see her cry, she let the grief flow through her.

Just an itty bitty experimental word play . . . how is GRIEVE different at the different times of day? Go on. Play!

_____

_____

CONTEMPLATE LIFE

She turned off the beeping alarm without hitting snooze, but she didn't get out of bed yet either. She just lay there for a moment in the broken sunlight to contemplate her life and prepare for the day.

Traffic hummed; people chatted; clocks chimed; wind whipped around corners. Standing alone in the hot sun, yet still surrounded by the busy bustle of the city, he paused and contemplated this life he had made for himself.

So I sat alone that night, with the darkness surrounding me, and truly contemplated life.

Just an itty bitty experimental word play . . . how is word different at the different times of day? Go on. Play!

_____

_____

THINK DIRTY THOUGHTS

She was certain she had a terrible case of bed head and terrible morning breath to match, but that didn't stop her from thinking about the dirty little things she wanted to try on him in the new morning light.

She walked past in her little skirt just short enough to be suggestive and just long enought to be proper. He hoped no one in the office noticed the dirty thoughts crossing his mind.

She lay there, waiting and fantasizing about what he could do to her. Dirty things. Good things.

Just an itty bitty experimental word play . . . how is word different at the different times of day? Go on. Play!

_____

_____

TALK TO YOURSELF

He grabbed his deodorant off the bathroom counter and shoved it in the bag with his razor and toothpaste. "Should that go in the clear ziplock?" he said, talking to himself, as he prepared for the two-day business trip. He was sure this used to be easier.

"I will not accept this kind of treatment," Rhonda went on talking to herself. "I am a professional and I deserve to be treated that way!" she finished with the flare she hoped she could hold onto in the real meeting with her boss.

Talking to himself, John said, "God, I think today was about all I could handle."

Just an itty bitty experimental word play . . . how is TALKING TO YOURSELF different at the different times of day? Go on. Play!

_____

_____

Doing

Check out these five doing happenings done at different times of the day.

MAKE A SANDWICH

He quickly threw some meat on sliced bread, shoved it in a plastic bag and ran out the door to catch the bus.

He was starving by noon. With only a half hour for lunch, he quickly made a sandwich and sat down at the table to eat.

He plowed through the fridge looking for the perfect late night snack. He found left over chicken, grabbed the mayonaise and made a quick sandwich before bed.

Just an itty bitty experimental word play . . . how is making a sandwich different at the different times of day? Go on. Play!

_____

_____

BREAK A PROMISE

She cursed under her breath. It was too early in the day to be breaking promises. But at least there were 18 hours left to make it up.

I had to. It was the right thing to do. What he was doing was wrong. He'll be better off in the end. He made me promise when I didn't want to. I knew my actions were justified but I still didn't feel any better about breaking that promise.

She promised not to see him again. A kiss here and a kiss there during the day seemed like nothing. But now, under the cover of night, these quick rendezvous seemed more passionate, and she knew her promise was broken.

Just an itty bitty experimental word play . . . how is breaking a promise different at the different times of day? Go on. Play!

EATING ICE CREAM

She felt just like a kid again as she ate her ice cream by the pool, quickly licking the drips before they dropped to the ground.

They took the kids for ice cream after dinner, just like they promised. Armed with napkins, they took their ice cream outside where the kids could eat their ice cream just like kids.

She walked through her apartment door, alone again, and went straight for the freezer. How stereotypically, she thought as she grabbed the Ben & Jerry's and began to eat.

Just an itty bitty experimental word play . . . how is word different at the different times of day? Go on. Play!

WALKING ON THE SIDEWALK

She walked down the sidewalk from her house and turned the corner. The air was crisp and the sun just starting to come up.

She walked down the sidewalk from her house and turned the corner. The mid-day heat was enough to make her wish she took the car instead.

She walked down the sidewalk from her house and turned the corner. It looked foreign in the dark of night and she felt slightly disoriented.

Just an itty bitty experimental word play . . . how is word different at the different times of day? Go on. Play!

_____

_____

DUST A COBWEB

That's the problem with being the first one out the door in the morning, he thought as he quickly dusted the cobweb from car door.

She absently dusted the cobwebs in the corner as she walked by, just as she did every day.

He dusted the cobweb from his car door with his bare and and involuntarily shuddered in the dark.

Just an itty bitty experimental word play . . . how is word different at the different times of day? Go on. Play!

_____

_____

Going

Check out these five going happenings done at different times of the day.

GO TO CHURCH

It was Sunday morning so they went to church, just like every Sunday.

He stepped hesitantly through the doors, unsure what to expect. He wasn't even sure what he was doing at church in the middle of the afternoon, to be honest. It just felt like the place he needed to be.

He went to church that night just to be there. He always felt safe and comforted within those walls. The silence gave him a chance to clear his mind and he prayed.

Just an itty bitty experimental word play . . . how is GOING TO CHURCH different at the different times of day? Go on. Play!

GO ON A DATE

It's just coffee, she told herself. It was a date, but it was just coffee. There's no implied commitment in morning coffee dates.

They met in the lobby for a quick lunch date as long as he was in the area.

She got dressed in the bedroom. He got ready in the bathroom. Sure they were married, but it was so rare that they got an evening alone. This was a date.

Just an itty bitty experimental word play . . . how is **GOING ON A DATE** different at the different times of day? Go on. Play!

_____

_____

AVOID SOMEONE

She woke up earlier than normal and hurried to leave the house. If she was quick, she could avoid everyone and get to her office in peace.

I could hear her coming around the corner. I was so busy that day. The last thing I wanted was another half hour of office gossip, so I ducked around the corner hoping I could avoid her.

Their house was small. You could only avoid someone for so long. She figured her best chance at avoiding him was to look busy, so she decided to carry the laundry basket from the bedroom down to the basement and back again. At least until he got in her way.

Just an itty bitty experimental word play . . . how is **AVOIDING SOMEONE** different at the different times of day? Go on. Play!

_____

_____

DRIVE

The morning glare was blinding as she drove along the highway.

He thought he left early enough to beat the rush, but traffic was barely moving on the highway.

There's barely any traffic on this stretch of highway at night so he was able to speed a majority of his way there.

Just an itty bitty experimental word play . . . how is **DRIVING** different at the different times of day? Go on. Play!

_____

_____

WINDOW SHOPPING

The stores weren't open yet, but she went to look anyway. No evil glares from the shop owners when you window shop before the stores are open.

She walked slowly past the storefronts imaging what it would be like to be able to shop at those kind of stores. She lingered a little longer at the shoe store window to pick out a new pair of heels, but her window shopping was interrupted by the salesman glaring back at her.

Everything was closed for the night, but she went to look anyway. She spent too much money shopping today anyway. Some window shopping would satisfy her for now.

Just an itty bitty experimental word play . . . how is **WINDOW SHOPPING** different at the different times of day? Go on. Play!

_____

_____

Word
Word Play!
Play
Word Play!
Word
Play
Play

Word
WORD PLAY!

90

WORD PLAY . . . YOUR Happenings in Time

Pick another thinking happening from the list to break down into morning, late day, and night sentences.

WORD:_____

Morning Sentence:

_____

_____

Late Day Sentence:

_____

_____

Night Sentence:

_____

_____

How is word different at the different times of day?

_____

_____

_____

Pick one of your own happening list thinking happenings from the list to break down into morning, late day, and night sentences.

WORD:_____

Morning Sentence:

_____

_____

Late Day Sentence:

_____

_____

Night Sentence:

_____

_____

How is word different at the different times of day?

_____

_____

_____

Pick another doing happening from the list to break down into morning, late day, and night sentences.

WORD:_____

Morning Sentence:

_____

_____

Late Day Sentence:

_____

_____

Night Sentence:

_____

_____

How is word different at the different times of day?

_____

_____

_____

Pick one of your own happening list doing happenings from the list to break down into morning, late day, and night sentences.

WORD:_____

Morning Sentence:

_____

_____

Late Day Sentence:

_____

_____

Night Sentence:

_____

_____

How is word different at the different times of day?

_____

_____

_____

Pick another going happening from the list to break down into morning, late day, and night sentences.

WORD:_____

Morning Sentence:

_____

_____

Late Day Sentence:

_____

_____

Night Sentence:

_____

_____

How is word different at the different times of day?

_____

_____

_____

Pick one of your own happening list going happenings from the list to break down into morning, late day, and night sentences.

WORD:_____

Morning Sentence:

_____

_____

Late Day Sentence:

_____

_____

Night Sentence:

_____

_____

How is word different at the different times of day?

_____

_____

_____

The
Happenings
Characterizations
The
Happenings
Characterizations
The

CHARACTERIZATIONS
Happenings

97

Happenings Characterizations

One way to establish a character is to tell it like it is. List the character's personality traits outright and present it directly to the reader. Directly setting out a character's personality definitely has its place and may, in some cases, be consistent with the character you are creating.

More often than not, however, at least the finer aspects of a character's personality are developed and communicated to a reader indirectly through the character's experiences, interactions and choices. Enter of happenings.

Different happenings *help you, the author, create memorable, relatable and emotionally complete characters. Whether a character acts through a thinking* happening *versus a doing* happening *helps create the character. Whether a character thinks a certain way in the morning versus at night helps create the character. Whether a character does certain activities at certain times of the day helps create the character. Heck, what a character doesn't do or doesn't think can be just as telling.*

If you're character is going to exist, and you're already proving it by letting the character engage in its happenings, *let the* happenings *work for you and build your character.*

Check out these five thinking happenings used to help create character.

Accept a Compliment

She didn't create the content, but it was her organization and layout and she did the talking. "Thanks," she replied, and this time truly accepted the compliment.

Just an itty bitty experimental word play . . . how does *"Accept a Compliment"* help to create layers and reality to your character?

_____

_____

_____

Dream

He was dreaming – flying, floating over the city, above green forests, past waterfalls so close he could feel the mist.

Just an itty bitty experimental word play . . . how does *"Dream"* help to create layers and reality to your character? Go on. Play!

_____

_____

_____

Flush

Just thinking about him made her flush.

Just an itty bitty experimental word play . . . how does *"Flush"* help to create layers and reality to your character? Go on. Play!

Lose Your Thought

The written words on the paper jumbled all together with the sounds coming from the TV and those of his own internal monologue….and he completely lost his train of thought.

Just an itty bitty experimental word play . . . how does *"Lose Your Thought"* help to create layers and reality to your character? Go on. Play!

Reminisce

Her grandpa's passing wasn't unexpected, but she still lay quietly in bed that night with a single happy tear the only outward sign of her reminiscing.

Just an itty bitty experimental word play . . . how does ***"Reminisce"*** help to create layers and reality to your character? Go on. Play!

_____

_____

_____

Check out these five doing happenings used to help create character.

Check the Weather

I felt the icy doorknob but still couldn't stop myself from sticking my head out the door to check the weather. Dang it was cold out this morning.

Just an itty bitty experimental word play . . . how does **"Check the Weather"** help to create layers and reality to your character? Go on. Play!

_____

_____

_____

Exhale

Closing his eyes he slowly exhaled while the scalding water ran down his back. Washing the dirt away was far easier than washing the emotional baggage he'd accumulated recently.

Just an itty bitty experimental word play . . . how does **"Exhale"** help to create layers and reality to your character? Go on. Play!

_____

_____

_____

Read a Menu

She read the menu for the third time while she waited for him to show up.

Just an itty bitty experimental word play . . . how does ***"Read a Menu"*** help to create layers and reality to your character? Go on. Play!

_____

_____

_____

Tease Someone

She sat down slowly and crossed her bare legs, teasing him with just enough skin. She brushed a stray lock of hair behind her ear, letting her finger trace her collar bone on the way back to her thigh. She knew what she was doing.

Just an itty bitty experimental word play . . . how does ***"Tease Someone"*** help to create layers and reality to your character? Go on. Play!

_____

_____

_____

Write Your Name

I wrote my name at the top of the page and waited for the proctor to give permission to rip open the exam book.

Just an itty bitty experimental word play . . . how does *"Write Your Name"* help to create layers and reality to your character? Go on. Play!

_____

_____

_____

Check out these five going happenings used to help create character.

Fly

Flying was the quickest and safest way to get there, but that didn't make the turbulence any more bearable.

Just an itty bitty experimental word play . . . how does *"Fly"* help to create layers and reality to your character? Go on. Play!

_____

_____

_____

Grocery Shop

Going grocery shopping was like a vacation hour from life. No tiny humans on this trip. Just aisles and aisles of organized shelves to slowly meander around while music softly played in the background.

Just an itty bitty experimental word play . . . how does *"Grocery Shop"* help to create layers and reality to your character? Go on. Play!

_____

_____

_____

Meet a Friend

*"Mom, just, like, stop here – I'll walk over. I don't want him to see you." "Him? I thought you were just meeting your friends." "He **is** a friend."*

Just an itty bitty experimental word play . . . how does **"Meet a Friend"** help to create layers and reality to your character? Go on. Play!

_____

_____

_____

Run

She felt an electrified tingle travel through her fingertips and set every nerve in her body on end as he grabbed her hand. "Run!" he said. And they ran.

Just an itty bitty experimental word play . . . how does **"Run"** help to create layers and reality to your character? Go on. Play!

_____

_____

_____

Take the Subway

Compared to driving, taking the subway was somewhat disorienting with all the dark passages, turns, noise and waves of people. Thanks goodness the signs were clearly visible at each platform.

Just an itty bitty experimental word play . . . how does *"Take the Subway"* help to create layers and reality to your character? Go on. Play!

_____

_____

_____

Word

Word Play!

Play

Word Play!

Word

Play

Play

Word
WORD PLAY!

Your Happenings Characterizations

Your turn to play! Pick one of your thinking happenings to create a passage that helps to create a strong character.

_____

_____

_____

_____

_____

_____

_____

_____

_____

_____

Your turn to play! Pick one of your doing happenings to create a passage that helps to create a strong character.

_____

_____

_____

_____

_____

_____

_____

_____

_____

_____

Your turn to play! Pick one of your going happenings to create a passage that helps to create a strong character.

_____

_____

_____

_____

_____

_____

_____

_____

_____

_____

_____

Passage
The
Happenings
Passage
The
Happenings
Passage
Happenings

The

The Happenings at Work

So you have some **happening** phrases, some idea of how these **happening** phrases provide thinking, doing and going actions, some thought of how the time of day changes the meaning or feel of these **happening** phrases, and some groundwork for a character. Now what?

At the risk of sounding like an elementary school teacher (sorry teachers, no offense), let's put it all together.

A character is just an idea – a thought, a concept, a disembodied imaginary friend (or acquaintance) (or….enemy) – until the character takes form. That is, until the character is put down on paper. Even then, if the character doesn't DO anything (or THINK anything, or GO anywhere) – if nothing happens to your character, who's to care about your character?

Use these happenings to develop your character into someone the reader cares about. Use these active phrases and manipulate the tone of the happening to suit your character. Use them to show your character's motivations. Use them to create a strong character and you're on your way to a story readers will devour.

Word
Word Play!
Play
Word Play!
Word
Play
Play

Word
Word Play!

Your Happenings at Work

We're jumping right to the wordplay on this one! Practice putting it all together and see how this little experiment has worked for you. We gave you the words (okay, and you supplied some, too). Now, it's time to PLAY: Create a passage that uses various thinking, going, and doing phrases, used at different times of day, to develop a unique character. Consider following your character through a single day and list all of his or her happenings, or, focus on a single part of the day to determine the best way to highlight how he or she . . . exists.

As Promised . . .

Overachievers, IGNITE! Yes, I know. Some of you really wanted more space for more happenings and I promised I'd supply some lined and blank pages. Well, I can overachieve, too! I've also provided a couple of our standard tables in case you want to do some of your own defining or categorizing for your happenings additions!

532. _____

533. _____

534. _____

535. _____

536. _____

537. _____

538. _____

539. _____

540. _____

541. _____

542. _____

543. _____

544. _____

545. _____

546. _____

547. _____

548. _____

549. _____

550. _____

551. _____

552. _____

553. _____

554. _____

555. _____

556. _____

557. _____

558. _____

559. _____

560. _____

561. _____

562. _____

563. _____

564. _____

565. _____

566. _____

567. _____

568. _____

569. _____

570. _____

571. _____

572. _____

573. _____

574. _____

575. _____

576. _____

577. _____

578. _____

579. _____

580. _____

581. _____

582. _____

583. _____

584. _____

585. _____

586. _____

587. _____

588. _____

589. _____

590. _____

591. _____

592. _____

593. _____

594. _____

595. _____

596. _____

597. _____

598. _____

599. _____

600. _____

Alright, alright! That's enough, already! The next pages include:

- Blank 2-Column Tables
- Blank 3-Column Tables
- Lined Note Pages
- Blank Note Pages

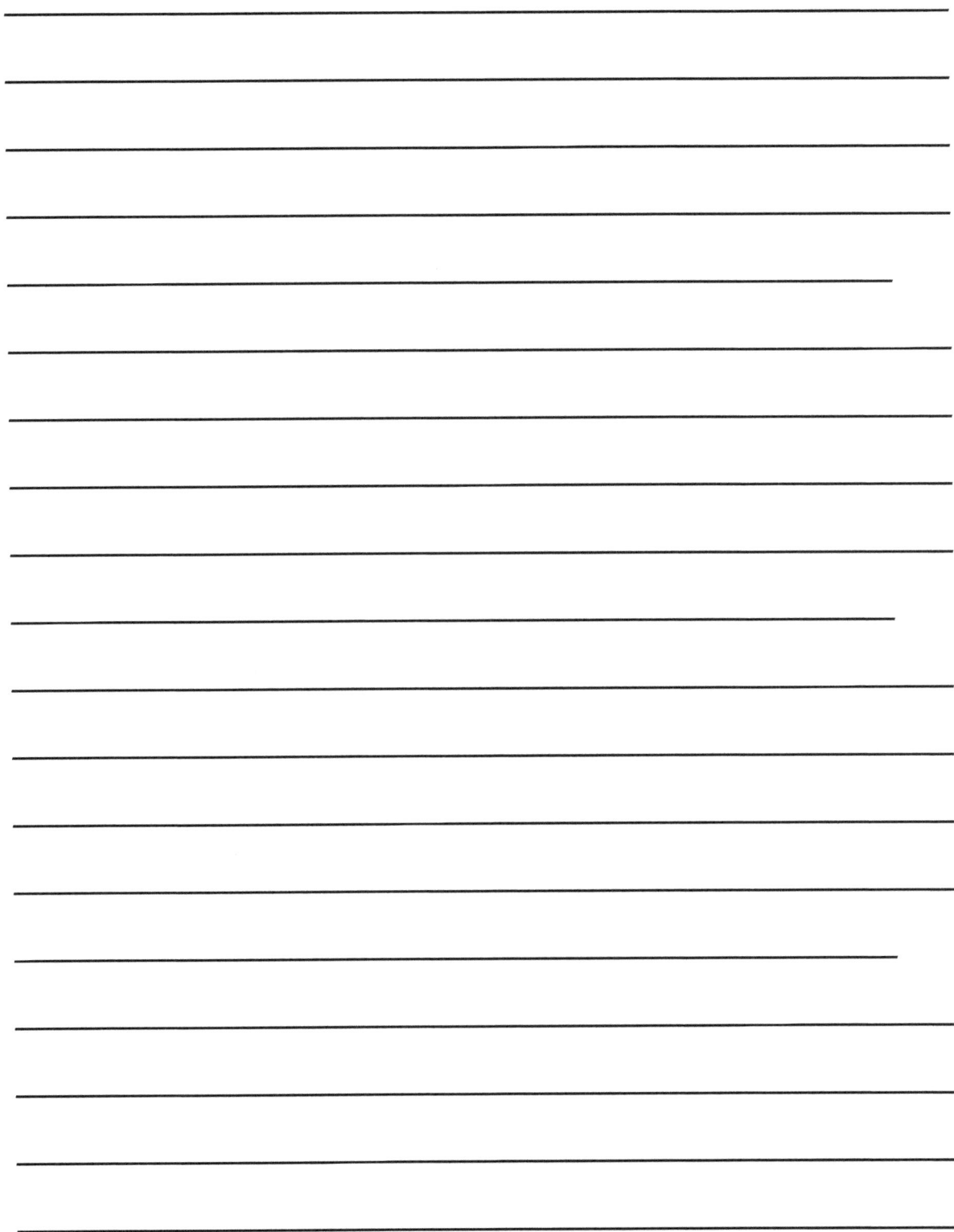

Afterword

Thanks for participating in this word experiment. Hopefully it was helpful.

Hopefully it was also meaningful.

The experiments you participated in revolved around the creation of a strong character and the creation of a strong story by recognizing the everyday activities — the everyday happenings — that all people (literary included) participate in on a daily basis. Seriously — were you keeping track? Is it possible to not check a single activity after just an hour? The experiments also showed how the same activity — the same happening — can be manipulated by you, the writer, to show a character's personality, motivations, background and even just plain old existence.

In the process, I hope you also came to realize that these happenings show a lot about YOU. What activities you participate in — what you think, what you do, and where you go — provide the world with a hint of you. Every how you think how you do, how you go. Every where you think, where you do, where you go. Every when you think, when you do, when you go. All of it shows the world a little bit more of you.

That puts a new perspective on making every moment count, right?

Even more than that — there may come a time when you feel like you don't want to or can't think or do or go. Whatever the reason, there could be a day when **any** happening seems impossible. The world will keep going, but you just want off. It's okay to take a break, but once that break is done and it's time to re-engage with the world . . . remember this list. Remember these active phrases. Remember these happenings. Put a check by all the thinkings, doings, and goings you complete for just one day.

Prove to yourself that you exist.

Resources Consulted

Online:
Merriam Webster Dictionary
Oxford English Dictionary
Dictionary.com
Thesaurus.com
Roget's Thesaurus

Experientially:
The Plays We've Experienced
The Books We've Read
The Movies We've Seen
The Songs We've Heard
The Conversations We've OVERheard

Cooperatively:
And Each Other

About the Authors

LAURA GREBE was born . . . arrived . . . was gifted to us on April 24th, 1985, her grandmother's namesake (oh! And Laura Holt from Remington Steele, too). Wife . . . spouse . . . betrothed . . . soul mate . . . other half to Josh Grebe and mother . . . mama . . . female parent . . . mommy . . . to Noah, the big brother Angel looking over his family from heaven, and Maddy, Noah's little sister.

A lifetime Wisconsinite and Patent Law lawyer living in the greater Milwaukee area, Laura knew she wanted to be a lawyer since the first grade when she started reading *Nancy Drew* books. She also loves science; reading (particularly mysteries with Nancy Drew and Sherlock Holmes being the favorites, science fiction, and tweeny-bopper mysteries and science fiction . . . um . . . *in German)*; scuba diving; jumping out of planes (attached to a qualified person wearing a parachute of course); baking cupcakes (aka: playing cupcake wars in her kitchen); showing Maddy the world; church; singing in the car (these days, usually to *Mickey Mouse Club*, *DocMcStuffins*, *Sofia the First*, and *Bubble Guppies*), and spending way too much money on Zulily and Shutterfly.

Laura's *500+ Happenings to Prove Existence*, *700+ Verbal Emojis*, and *1000+ Still Useful Words* were born out of her *Maternity Journal*. (Stay tuned! It's coming; we promise!) Through the unimaginable loss of a son that occurred before her pregnancy with Maddy, she and her husband, Josh, recognized the impossible relatability of journals to a grieving person who fearfully hopes and anticipates new life. Being often laid up during Maddy's prenatal days, Laura found herself digging deeper than ever to place intentional recognition on the things she did, felt, and observed. To Laura, these lists were tools to help her describe her days' experiences, but her publisher realized that, to the writers and the therapeutic writing journalists they routinely work with, Laura's simple tools were anything but. So came the *Experimental Word Play* series that she now brings you.

She promises the venture into list-land won't change the uniqueness of her, punctuated by decided favorites that keep her connecting to the world and its words including: *animal* – bunny; *salty snack* - popcorn or Tostitos; *sweet snack* – cupcakes (we can't wait to bring you her *Cupcake Therapy* book!); *time of day* - morning sunrise; *season* – fall; *holiday* – Halloween; *color* - green (but not lime green, green green or olive green - more like leafy, natural green); *sport* – soccer; *dream vacation* – London; *drink* – iced tea; *clothing style* – classic, hippy, and/or old-school pin-up (you know, the kind that was sexy but didn't really show anything by today's standards); *music* – country; and *lucky number* – 13, which is how many favorites are listed here!

Working with Laura to create the *Experimental Word Play* series was **REJI LABERJE**, Owner and Creative Director of Reji Laberje Writing and Publishing. Reji is a Bestselling Author with nineteen years of professional-level experience in the writing industry and her fortieth book hitting the presses in 2016. Laura's creativity was a joy for Reji to embrace. She looks forward to using the 500+, 700+, and 1000+ for the 20,000+ days she would be lucky to have left on God's green Earth. Also in that time, she intends to continue living life outside of Milwaukee where she resides with her husband of twenty years, Joe, and their active family of seven people and four pets.

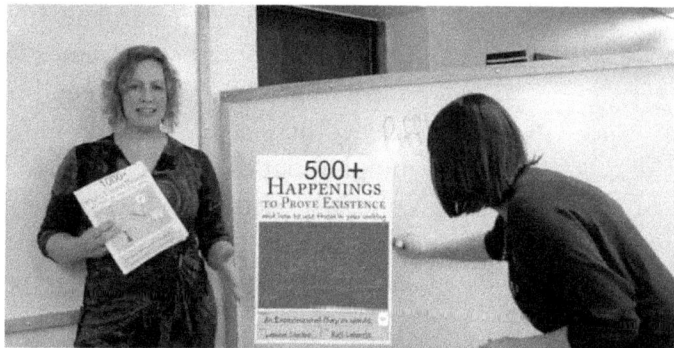

(Laura and Reji introduce their experimental word play series.)

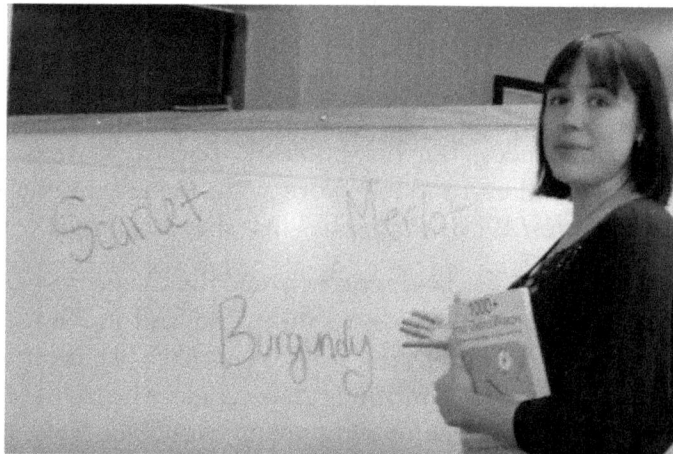

(Laura plays with colors from "1000+ Still Useful Words.)

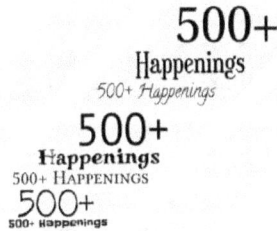

500+
Happenings
500+ Happenings
500+
Happenings
500+ HAPPENINGS
500+
500+ Happenings

Happenings

And remember to check out the ERH as I'm pretty sure there will be addendums and additions coming to all of the Experimental Word Play lists!

Happenings . . . hmm . . .

1. **Miss Your Step** (trip, fall, stumble, foot stutter) – Doing/Going
2. **Take a Swig** (take a large swallow of a drink) - Doing
3. **Feel Sexy** (do something or put on something that makes one feel worthy of attention, typically from the other sex, regardless of how others, including the opposite sex, felt toward that individual prior to the doing or putting on of something) - Thinking
4. **Feel Smart** (do something that makes one feel intelligent or exhibit confidence, regardless of that individual's actual intelligence level) - Thinking
5. **Cut Yourself** (nick, scrape, damage the skin, usually with a piece of paper, usually requiring at least five plasters before the bleeding stops) - Doing
6. **Clean Glasses** (wipe greasy fingerprints off spectacles) - Doing
7. **Get Gas** (fill up a car or other gas-guzzling vehicle) – Doing/Going

I'm continuing . . . I hope you'll come play, too!

Laura Grebe – Electronic Resource Hub
www.rejilaberje.com/laura-grebe.html

133

500+
HAPPENINGS
TO PROVE EXISTENCE
and how to use them in your writing

SUBJECT
An Experim

WITH
Laura Gre

700+
VERBAL EMOJIS
and how to use them in your writing

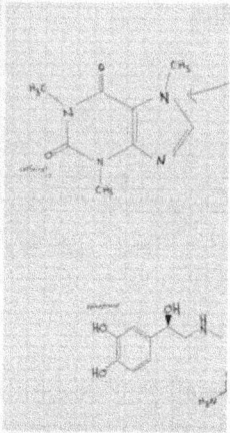

SUBJECT
An Experime

WITH
Laura Greb

1000+
STILL USEFUL WORDS
and how to use them in your writing

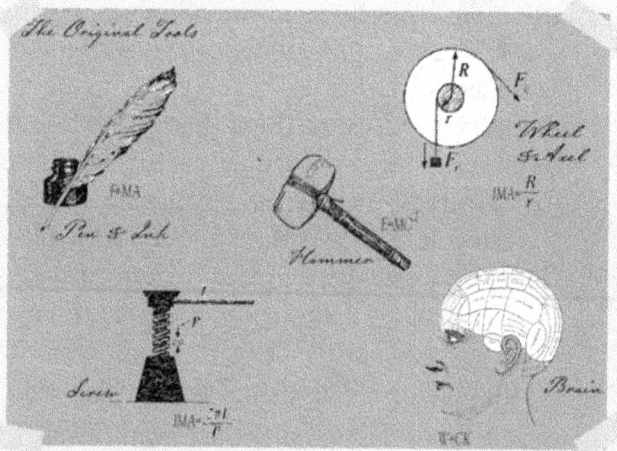

SUBJECT
An Experimental Play on Words   03

WITH
Laura Grebe   AND   Reji Laberje